FINANCIAL SURVIVAL

for Families in the Grip of

DEMENTIA

I0137151

KERRY MORRIS, CFP®, CFEd®

This book is being given to

_____

because I care about helping you and your family.

ISBN: 978-1-948261-91-3

Interior Layout & Formatting: Ronda Taylor, heartworkcreative.com

Hugo House Publishers, Ltd.
Austin, TX • Denver, CO
HugoHousePublishers.com

Dedication

This book is dedicated to three specific groups of people.

1. The adult children, caregivers, and spouses of aging individuals, who lost a loved one from COVID-19 during the pandemic. our hearts and prayers are with you.
2. The adult children, caregivers and spouses of aging individuals who are still fighting the good fight. Whether you are caring for a loved one who is confusing the microwave with the oven due to dementia, or you are helping your parent shower and dress each morning, your efforts do not go unnoticed.
3. This book is also dedicated to the incredible group of elder law attorneys, geriatric care managers, care community workers and financial advisors who have made it their passion to help families navigate the rough waters as they try to provide quality long-term care for their loved one without going broke in the process in a post COVID-19 world.

If you are reading this book, it has most likely been provided to you as a resource from one of these remarkable individuals.

Contents

Acknowledgments

I have had the pleasure of seeing every one of these programs improve a family's journey by helping them access and afford more and better care for a loved one in one way or another. I would like to express my deepest gratitude to all the mentors, colleagues, company reps, actuaries, insurance and government program creators, caregiver trainers, and thought leaders who helped create and expose me to all these amazing options that we have collected into one toolbox of this book. There are too many people to list individually. When I think of the amount of energy and effort it took across several industries and the government to create all these amazing solutions to help people it's mind boggling.

However, there are some specific people who I want to mention:

My amazing wife and children who are a gift to me that I continue to unwrap daily. What an adventure.

Tyrone Clark for having the same vision and commitment to take this message to the world. Your partnership, forty-plus years of experience, off-the-charts creative thinking, and the faith we share in Jesus means the world to me. I look forward to taking this journey together.

My staff, Kelly Martin, and Austin Morris, who put up with me being so picky about everything.

My mom and dad who taught me to never give up and to always find and fight for the bright side.

The hundreds of families that entrusted me to help them navigate Longevity Care Allocation Planning for their loved ones and all the Care Providers that sent them to come to see me. Without those experiences, I would not have known to look beyond the money to understand the real cost families pay when the money is running out.

Introduction

The problem was right there. There was never enough money. People who had elderly parents, wives who were taking care of their husbands (or vice versa), or good friends who were concerned about their friend or neighbor, or if they were the appointed caregiver, it didn't matter. They were all there because they heard that maybe—hopefully—I could help them.

This was in 2010, and I was deep in the trenches of elder-care planning. I felt for them. I had become an investment advisor and founded Assurance Financial Partners two years prior. Still, because I was doing more and more elder-care planning, I opened the Estate and Elder Planning Center a year earlier in Franklin, Tennessee. By the end of that year, the volume of people asking for help with their elder-care planning had become so great that I focused on their issues for the next two years.

As an investment advisor, my job is to help people mindfully grow their money, make sure their risk tolerance is well-heeded, and plan carefully to ensure they have the right portfolio mix and income streams. My goal always is for my clients to have a great retirement.

By 2012, I had decided to turn my focus back to helping people retire successfully. But after what I had seen in the trenches of elder-care planning, I knew every plan had to include something that would provide extra money from outside the portfolio should they need to pay for care not covered by Medicare as they aged.

It was tough when I went back to investment advising, but I made sure that every client we worked with included a plan to handle what I quickly came to call the "ticking time bomb" in pretty much everyone's investment portfolio. It was a defect of massive proportions because I also realized, fairly quickly, that the financial planning and investment advising community—my chosen profession—had been asleep at the wheel. Because when that bomb went off, the portfolio was no longer just "defective," it was decimated, and all the hard work my clients and I did together to preserve their wealth would be wasted.

Pretty much everyone is now aware of the "triple threat" of retirement. This is what happens to your money when you have (1) market losses, combined with (2) income withdrawals, and you have to (3) pay taxes on that money (not to mention inflation). But what about the cost of care? I had witnessed the triple threat turn into a quadruple nightmare. When the cost of care depletes a portfolio, the market losses, income withdrawals, and taxes become so magnified that even the most robust portfolios can be crippled or wiped out.

Those people who all came to see me years before had watched tens of thousands of dollars flow out of their accounts for care. They were dealing with this deadly combination of the "triple threat" and rising care costs.

And it wasn't just a mom issue or a dad issue. It really was a family issue. Someone had to take care of Mom or Dad or Auntie Jill or Johnny, the old guy who lived next door and was a confirmed bachelor. Someone had to pay for it with either human or financial capital, and usually both.

By the way, Medicare doesn't pay for the everyday stuff—the help getting out of bed, eating, getting dressed for the day, going to the bathroom, brushing teeth, and getting back into bed at the end of the day. The only way Medicaid pays a dime is if you don't have any money left to handle the cost and you need to put your loved one in a Medicaid skilled nursing home.

That's the end result of the dreaded Medicaid spend-down. So when you add "cost of care" to the triple threat, it becomes the quadruple nightmare. But how could a family handle this?

I had originally started working with traditional long term care insurance. Historically, this has been the "go-to" for pretty much everyone. But that solution, while sometimes workable, inherently has two major problems that most people don't like, and neither do I. It is a "use it or lose it" proposition, and the price is never locked in. Because of that, insurance carriers were handing out CRAZY premium increases. Those people who were insured had to pay a lot more for the same benefits, and new policies were stripped of several advantages, like the lifetime payout option.

As a guy who thought in terms of the roles that each piece of a client's plan would play in their retirement success, I wanted to find a solution that would allow us to allocate a portion of someone's nest egg to produce more of a win-win than what I was seeing in traditional long term-care insurance. I guess I could say that the win-win I was looking for found me. Once I found the optimum solution, I began to include it in all the plans I was building to help clients transition into retirement, and they loved it. They had no idea solutions like these existed.

I thought, "Hey, we should build a class to show people what's really going on in this industry and why this solution is really the best one. It will be great!"

It went over like a proverbial lead balloon. People didn't show up. I had failed to realize how much the public simply didn't want to talk about it back then. Ten years ago, most people could only think of traditional long term care insurance and nursing homes when they saw this topic. Even more than today, people were used to being reactive, meaning they waited until the problem was practically insurmountable before they decided to do something about it. That's how this long-term care problem had been handled for decades. But when it comes to paying for care, it's almost always too late when you are reactive

This is why investment advisors aren't aware of what they can do to help their clients with this issue. Insurance and annuity agents often turn a blind eye because anytime anyone even hints at "longevity planning" or "long-term care," everyone immediately thinks of traditional long term care insurance. Although the tide has been changing gradually, for some of them, it is still the most dreaded conversation they have with a client.

Compared to what people should know, this solution is still hidden. But the impetus that made me create that first class for people never left me. I have a duty to share what I know with the world. Hence, *Financial Survival for Families in the Grip of Dementia*.

We live in a time that everyone knew was coming: all the baby boomers are now birthday-ing themselves into their golden years. But that's actually only half the story. One of my favorite books, *The Longevity Economy*, is very clear. The other half is the ever-lowering birth rate. More and more people live into their late eighties and nineties, but we're not getting the corresponding increase in the workforce. It's a blessing on one hand and a national problem on the other because neither this generation nor this country is prepared financially. And it's not going to get better unless families take matters into their own hands and plan ahead.

The government isn't going to fix it. The truth is, Medicare is taking care of less and less as the cost of care goes up and up. So the only answer is to take care of you and yours now.

I call the solution I found the LCAP—Longevity Care Allocation Planning. It is proactive, meaning you aren't waiting until you need it to get it. It cures the defective portfolio syndrome that I saw plague pretty much everyone's portfolio. You put it in place long before you feel your joints starting to creak, you can't dress yourself, and your short-term memory is getting spotty, at best.

It has also proven itself to truly be a win-win over the past decade. You have it if you need it; it's not wasted if you don't. In other words, you can grow a leveraged pool of money specifically for your care in your later years, and your heirs get the money if you don't use it. But it's not traditional long term care insurance.

Curious? Read on.

The Long-Term Care Crisis

A Close Look at the Numbers: The Cost of Care

The biggest and most obvious question for seniors and for long-term care needs is usually money. How are we going to pay for long-term care? **According to Genworth*, in 2022 the cost of care looked like this:**

- The national average daily rate for a private room in a nursing home was $297 while the daily rate for a semi-private room was $260.
- The national average monthly base rate in an assisted-living community was $4,500.
- The national average hourly rate for home health aides was $27; for homemakers it was $26. The national average daily rate for adult day services was $78.

* *The 2022 Genworth Cost of Care Survey; Home Care Providers, Adult Day Health Care Facilities, Assisted Living Facilities and Nursing Homes*

Privately paying for long-term care means that seniors would have to find an additional $50,000 to $130,000 per year in their budget for just ONE person to receive care. Most of us, seniors or not, could not afford to privately pay for our own care year after year.

Long-term care insurance will pay for in-home care, assisted living, and nursing-home care. This is the most appropriate and needed form of insurance protection available to us today. Long-term care insurance should be termed "lifestyle" insurance—it is NOT nursing-home insurance! If your vision of your later years includes sitting at home in your own recliner, with your own remote control, watching your own TV...well, you should be planning for that future with long-term care insurance. In later chapters we discuss all of the options related to long-term care insurance today, since the COVID-19 pandemic the new guaranteed issue Long Term care options now available..

Reverse mortgages (Home Equity Conversion Mortgages) have become one of the most popular and accepted ways of paying for many different expenses, including the cost of long-term care. Reverse mortgages are designed to keep seniors at home longer. A reverse mortgage can pay for in-home care, home repair, home modification, and any other need a senior may have. Almost every successive chapter in this book discusses the use of reverse mortgages for seniors in some way. That is how important this cash flow planning concept has become in recent years.

Government Assistance

Medicaid will pay for long-term care, but certain criteria must be met. It is important to seek the advice of a qualified financial professional and an elder law attorney prior to applying for Medicaid.

Veterans Directed Care: A new program that allows the veteran to have a level of choice regarding from whom they receive care.

VA Aid and Attendance Pension Benefit: The VA Aid and Attendance Pension Benefit is available to certain Veterans and their spouses who served during a period of war. Both Medicaid and VA Aid and Attendance are discussed later in the book.

Who Is Going to Take Care of Mom and Dad?

According to a recent joint study conducted by Cornell and Purdue University and supported by the National Institute on Aging, aging mothers are nearly four times more likely to expect a daughter to assume the role of their caregiver rather than a son if they become ill or disabled. According to AARP* 1in 5 Americans, or over 53 million Americans provide unpaid family care.

These mothers are also much more likely to choose a child to whom they feel emotionally close and who has values similar to their own, according to Karl Pillemer, Professor of Human Development at Cornell, and Purdue sociologist Jill Suitor, in the journal, *The Gerontologist.*[1]

Aging adults today who are on the threshold of needing additional assistance in the home are also aging adults who tended to have larger families during their childbearing years. It is important, though often difficult, for seniors to talk with their adult children about expectations and wishes. It is also important for adult children to talk with each other about who will be assuming what role with regard to helping Mom and Dad. Neglecting to discuss this at all can lead to disappointment, confusion, and disagreement between siblings.

Long-term care is a family issue, but it is more often a woman's issue. Throughout history women have been the caregivers in our lives. As we have seen, women also live longer than men on average. From beginning to end, women often care for family members young and old. Now, as our population begins to age, it is even more important that we understand what lies before us.

---

1   **The Gerontologist** 46:439-448 (2006) © 2006 The Gerontological Society of America Making Choices: A Within-Family Study of Caregiver Selection Karl Pillemer, PhD1, and J. Jill Suitor, PhD

Although we see the number of male caregivers increasing all the time, the fact remains that, when it comes to long-term care for our family members and our spouses, today women carry the weight.

Daughters, daughters-in-law, wives, sisters and nieces often accept the role of caregiver for aging adults in the family. Across the U.S. there are women commonly referred to as "the sandwich generation" who are playing dual roles in their families. They are often mothers themselves in addition to caring for their own aging parents. The level of stress and frustration can be overwhelming. Careers are being put on hold, and promotions passed up, in order to accommodate the busy schedules of their children and their parents. Even so, there is still not enough time for these women to meet everyone's needs. A financial burden results as well. This is why since COVID-19 more caregivers are taking advantage of the Consumer Directed Care program through Medicaid that allows family members to receive compensation for providing care to loved ones.

Women in America also tend to marry men who are older than they are. Therefore, they often end up caring for a chronically ill spouse in later years. When this happens, it is sometimes the case that all of the retirement funding and assets are used to pay for the long-term care needs of the "ill" spouse, leaving nothing in savings to care for the "well" spouse later in life.

It is estimated that one out of every two women will need long-term care at some point in their lives. One of every three men will also require long-term care. So why do more women need services? A woman's life expectancy is still longer than that of the average male.

How Long Can Seniors Be Cared for at Home—Realistically?

The answer to this question depends on many things, but ultimately it depends on how much support seniors have in their own community from family, friends, neighbors and religious organizations, and their ease of access to the medical system. Cash flow, as previously discussed, is another factor that determines how long seniors can stay at home safely.

It is important to note that according to a study by the National Association of Home Builders 50+ Housing Council, for those owning single family homes, 35.9% of households in the 55 to 64 age group reported difficulty in at least one physical activity:

- difficulty in dressing (9%)
- vision or hearing difficulty (11%)
- difficulty in going out (11.9%)
- difficulty in walking, reaching, lifting, carrying, climbing stairs or getting around the house (27.1%)
- difficulty in remembering (12.7%)
- and difficulty in working (23.8%)

More than 45% of those 65 to 74 and 70% of households 75 or older reported difficulty in some activity.[2]

Set up properly, a senior can stay in his or her own home for their entire life. As long as care can be paid for, or provided by family members locally, and as long as the living situation is safe and comfortable, seniors can stay at home. In the next few chapters we will give you more information on how this can be achieved.

---

2   March 2007, National Association of Home Builders 50+ Housing Council Study— Aging Boomers May Be Hard to Budge From Current Homes

Where Will Your Aging Parent Receive Care?

Choosing the Right Home Care Agency

The most desirable choice for many families is to keep an aging loved one at home for as long as possible. Assuming that is the case, here are some tips on choosing a home care agency.

- Be organized.
- Ask the Home Care Agency if they have a back-up person on call in case of caregivers becoming ill or not showing up.
- Provide the aide with a checklist of duties for EACH DAY.
- The aide should not sleep or smoke in your home.
- If there is a problem, immediately contact the agency that sent the aide.
- The aides should provide their own lunch/dinner unless you offer.
- Do not tip.
- Do not send your loved one out in a car with the aide unless this situation is prearranged with the agency.
- Aides should only minimally use the phone for personal calls.

- Make sure you know in advance how payment is expected.
- Some aides are Certified Nurse's Aides (CNAs) and others are not. Some will take a blood pressure and a pulse while others will not. Ask the agency.
- There should be some consistency after about 1 to 2 weeks regarding the person who is sent to the home. Sometimes it takes a week or so to get the same person on the schedule for your home. Be patient!
- What is the hiring practice of the agency? Have background checks been performed on every caregiver? What about Elder Abuse or Child Abuse database checks? Are they bonded and insured?
- If there are too many late shows/no shows or inconsistencies, CHANGE AGENCIES (speak to them about the problem first, perhaps they can correct the situation).

Medical vs. Non-Medical Home Care Services

There are two different types of home-care providers, **medical** and **non-medical**. A non-medical home-care agency supplies caregivers who will do household chores such as light cleaning, laundry, errand running, grocery shopping, picking up prescriptions, light meal preparation and getting the mail. They will also provide services that help with socialization and transportation like accompanying the aging adult to a doctor's appointment, sitting and watching TV together, playing card games or board games, taking the senior to special events or senior centers, going to the library, and other social activities. Again, transporting the senior in the care-giver's vehicle should be pre-approved.

In addition, non-medical home-care providers can also provide bathing and dressing assistance, medication reminders, and assistance with transferring from the bed to a chair. Medical home-care provides physical, occupational and speech therapy as well as wound care.

No one can take care of your parent or spouse exactly the way you would, but a good agency will provide caring and compassionate staff who do the best job they possibly can. The squeaky wheel always gets the grease when it comes to service providers. Do your homework prior to hiring an agency, and be sure to check on your aging loved one regularly. Visit unexpectedly and monitor what is happening in the home. Speak up and communicate with the agency!

Choosing an Adult Day Services Center

Adult day care centers are becoming a popular alternative to nursing home placement. They offer the ability for the elderly to spend the day in an enriching environment, full of social activities and learning opportunities, while interacting with others. Many adult day care centers will provide transportation to and from the center for an extra charge. Meals are provided, as well as medication administration. Day trips, crafts, computer stations, libraries and music are often part of the overall experience. Some adult day care centers will take Medicaid, but most prefer private pay or long-term care insurance. This allows the senior to live at home with another member of the family, but have supervision and social interaction during the day while family members are at work.

Tips for Choosing an Adult Day Services Center

- **Identify services in your area.** For names and phone numbers of the adult day care centers, try:
- **Computer** (Google Search "Adult Day Care;" "Aging Services;" Senior Citizens' Services," etc. near me).
  — **Area Agency on Aging (AAA).** Call 1-800-677-1116 for the AAA in your area, or search for them on-line.
    › A local senior center.
    › Your family doctor.
    › A Geriatric Care Manager.

- **Call first!** Call adult day care centers and ask for a flier or brochure, eligibility criteria, a monthly activity calendar, a monthly menu and application procedures.
- **Know what to ask.** Look for the following information:
  — **Owner or sponsoring agency.**

  — **Years of operation.**

  — **Openings and availability.** Are they accepting new clients?

  — **License or certification** (if required in your state).

  — **Hours of operation.**

  — **Days open.**

  — **Transportation.**

  — **Cost.** Hourly or daily charge, other charges, financial assistance.

  — **Medical conditions accepted.** Such as memory loss, limited mobility, and incontinence.

  — **Staff credentials.**

  — **Number of staff per participant.**

  — **Activities provided.** Is there variety and choice of individual and group activities?

  — **Menu.** Appeal, balance.

  — **Tour.** After reviewing materials, make an appointment to visit two or more centers that might meet your needs.

  — **Check references.** Talk to two or three people who have used the center you are considering. Ask for their opinion.

— **Try it out.** Select a day center. Try it for three to five days. It sometimes takes several visits for new participants to feel comfortable in a new setting and with a new routine. If you have questions or are experiencing any problems, ask for a conference. The staff may have suggestions for making the transition easier, both at home and at the day center.

Choosing an Assisted-Living Facility

Sometimes there are assisted-living facilities on the same campus with independent living that offer most of the same accommodations but with a little more assistance and structure. In an assisted-living facility, each resident typically has their own apartment but without a kitchenette. They are served three meals per day in a family-style or restaurant-style setting. Medication delivery is available, as well as linen service, laundry service, housekeeping, and assistance with bathing and dressing if needed. Again, recreation, social activities and transportation are also provided.

There are stand-alone assisted-living facilities that are not associated with Continuous Care Retirement Communities (CCRCs). Assisted living is becoming the most popular form of long-term care and is seen as a transition between independent living and nursing-home care. This is a nice option for people who need some extra help but are not ready for full 24-hour care. The cost of assisted-living ranges from $2,800-$12,000 per month and can be paid for with private funds or long-term care insurance.

Nursing Home Care

When independent or assisted living is no longer a viable option, a nursing home will provide 24-hour care by trained and licensed staff. A Registered Nurse or Licensed Practical Nurse is on duty at all times. Some nursing homes are private pay only, some take

Medicare for a limited period of time and some will accept Medicaid as payment for services. Most residents live in a semi-private room (private if they can afford it), and are allowed to decorate with their own personal belongings. There are new trends in nursing-home care called The Eden Alternative ™. These programs incorporate living things like plants, animals and children into residential care facilities to make them more like a home, rather than an institution for the frail and elderly. The average cost for a semi-private nursing home bed nationwide in 2021 was around $260 per day ($7,908 per month) or more.

Tips for Choosing an Assisted-Living or Nursing-Care Facility

Choosing a facility for a loved one, or even for yourself, can be difficult and time-consuming. The following tips and hints will help give you guidance when trying to make that decision. Remember—take notes on each facility you visit and compare them later. Anticipating your loved one's need for nursing home care will be very important, especially if your loved one has dementia, since many dementia units have waiting lists that can range from 6 to 18 months.

- Speak with people you trust about their experiences with nursing homes.
- Pick a good LOCATION.
- Ask the home about BED AVAILABILITY.
- Do they have Medicare, Medicaid, or private pay beds available?
- What is the STAFFING ARRANGEMENT? RNs? LPNs? CNAs?
- Are there extra services and fees?
- Is the home able to provide for special care needs such as Alzheimer's, End Stage Renal Disease, or other medical conditions?

- VISIT THE HOMES ON YOUR LIST! Nothing replaces a tour.
- Ask to see a copy of the most recent state inspection, or visit the Nursing Home Compare site on the web at **www.medicare. gov.**
- Do the residents seem to have a good quality of life?
- How long has the current staff been working at the facility?
- Does the facility conduct background checks for criminal and elder abuse activity prior to hiring employees?
- Upon entering the facility, pay attention to what you SEE and what you SMELL.
- What are the visiting hours?
- Security? Safety plans for fire evacuations etc.?
- Be sure to visit the home at least once when they are not expecting you.
- Make an inventory of the items that you or your loved one bring to the home for future reference. It would also be a good idea to label everything, such as canes, wheelchair, walker, etc.
- Talk to some of the other visitors/family members. How do they feel about the care provided?

Adult Children and Family Members Caring for an Aging Adult— Give Yourself a Break

When the Caregiver Needs a Break… Where Can They Turn?

One out of every four families in the U.S. today are caring for an aging adult in some way. For some families, that means 24-hour live-in care. For other families, that means that Mom needs a ride to the doctor or to the grocery store.

Over the last 10 years, it is projected that elder care will replace childcare as the number one issue for working adults. Employers have likewise been.

Caring for an aging parent can be rewarding and overwhelming at the same time. After all, these are one's parents who raised and cared for us. It is very difficult when the roles reverse.

Respite (res-pit) care is often the answer. Respite care is *time off* for the caregiver. Respite gives the caregiver time away to rest and do necessary activities so that they can continue to provide good care for their loved one. Being a caregiver is often a job that can be physically and emotionally draining. Without relief, a person's physical and emotional health can be affected, reducing the quality of care for their family member. There are several options when it comes to respite care.

In-home care can be arranged for as little as a few hours, up to several days with the proper planning and financial resources. Be sure to pick an agency with a great reputation and proven reliability. Make sure that background checks are done on all employees and Elder/Child Abuse checks are also completed. In-home care for long periods of time can be costly, so be sure to budget for the expense. Also many home health agencies require several days or weeks of advance notice for long assignments. Plan ahead!

Nursing-Care/Assisted-Living facilities will often offer respite care for a weekend or a full week or more. Many facilities have a minimum number of days required. The cost includes room and board; many other services will be extra. Some facilities will only require a few day's notice, and others will require several week's notice. Check with the facilities in your area for costs and bed availability. As always, it is important to plan ahead.

Local Area Agencies on Aging or Social Service Agencies will sometimes sponsor programs that allow for volunteers to come to the home and provide respite care for short periods of time. These visits are usually just for a few hours. The volunteers are not medical professionals and therefore are not able to care for seriously ill family members, but they are able to provide some relief! These programs are usually free or at a very low cost to local residents. Contact your local Area Agency on Aging for more information.

The Alzheimer's Association is a great source of information. It is not necessary to be taking care of an Alzheimer's- diagnosed family member to take advantage of their referral database. Your local agency can usually provide you with a wealth of information, resources and contacts.

Family and friends are a great resource for the caregiver. Do not be afraid to ask for help; many people are happy to assist with errand running and care-giving. Have a family meeting and ask each family member for 1-2 hours of his or her time per week; this will allow the caregiver to take a hot bath, read a book, go for a much-needed walk, or just go shopping. Make a schedule and give each family member a copy.

Local Churches and Other Organizations are generally willing to send volunteers out to the home for a few hours. Again, most of these volunteers are non-medical personnel and will only be able to stay for a couple of hours at a time.

Taking care of yourself is just as important as caring for your disabled/aging family member. If you become ill, what will happen to your loved one? Do not hesitate to ask for help. If you look in the right places, you might find more help than you need.

So take a much-needed break. You deserve it!

Hospice Care—at the End of Life

Hospice care is end-of-life care. Usually, it is estimated by a physician that a patient has 6 months or less to live. Hospice focuses on caring for the individual, keeping them comfortable, and providing support for the family. Hospice care can be provided in the home, in a designated hospice facility, or in a long-term care facility. These services are available to patients of all ages. It is covered under Medicare, Medicaid, and most private insurance plans. Long-term care insurance also covers hospice care.

The primary caregiver for a hospice patient is usually a family member. There is a team of healthcare professionals available to help the primary caregiver; this team often includes a physician, a registered nurse, home health aides, clergy or social services, trained volunteers, and physical or occupational therapists. Traditional insurance plans like Medicare and private health insurance will cover needed supplies, equipment, and licensed healthcare practitioners like nurses and physical therapists. However, when a family needs 24 hour care provided by a home health aide, or other unlicensed personnel, they end up paying privately for this service or utilizing their long-term care insurance benefits. Most long-term care insurers provide hospice care as a standard benefit in their plan and there is no need to meet the waiting period (elimination period).

Pay Yourself or a Loved One for Providing Care—The Options and Tax Benefits

Many adult children find it financially impossible to leave their current employer and give up a much needed salary to take care of an aging adult. There are some ways to offset that financial responsibility, but it does take diligence and investigation on the part of the adult child.

Seniors can pay adult children or other care providers, just like they would a home health agency for services, by using a care-giver's contract. This document can be drafted by an elder law attorney.

Some seniors have long-term care insurance that allows a family member to be the primary caregiver and get reimbursed for providing the care.

Guaranteed Issue Long Term Care Annuities are now available that conform to the Pension Protection Act. These annuities allow you to withdraw tax-free benefits from the account and pay friends or family members for your care at home. (See example in chapter 8).

- **NEW immediate annuities that are individually underwritten for individuals who are already receiving Long-Term Care. These annuities may allow the insured to**

receive significantly more income than a normal annuity once they are unable to do 2 of the 6 activities of daily living like eating, dressing, bathing, continence, toileting and transferring; or they are in cognitive decline caused by dementia. (see example in chapter 9)

- Medicaid now allows under the Consumer Directed Care program for individuals who are on Medicaid to have family members provide care at home and get paid from Medicaid. (see your trusted advisor for more information)
- Veterans Directed Care is a program that allows veterans who are in need of care to receive their care at home by a friend or family member and have the person providing the care services to be paid by the Veterans Administration.(see your trusted advisor for more information)

Tax Deductions and Benefits for Caregivers

There are certain criteria that must be met if a family caregiver is planning to claim an aging parent as a dependent.

1. You must provide more than half of a person's financial support.
2. The dependent may be a relative or non-relative living with you for the entire year or residing in a nursing home or assisted-living home.
3. The dependent must be a citizen of the U.S., Canada, or Mexico.
4. The dependent must not file a joint tax return for the same year.

Qualifying expenses include:

1. Medications
2. Long-term care insurance premiums
3. Home modifications

4. Transportation for medical appointments
5. Services of privately hired in-home care workers
6. Spending for wheelchairs, eye glasses, and dentures
7. Look for anything related to meeting the long-term care needs of the individual! Any expense not covered by insurance may be eligible for deductions.
8. For those residing in an assisted-living facility, there may be a certain percentage allowed as deductions.
9. For those residing in a nursing home—and paying privately for their care, the cost is fully deductible.

It is important to consult a tax advisor or elder law attorney, especially if the support gets complicated—for instance:

- When multiple siblings contribute to the support of a parent.
- When taxable income could be moved into tax-free investments.
- When there is the possibility that the dependent may need to apply for Medicaid.
- When a caregiver contract is desired to provide family members with compensation for services, housing, etc.

If you hired someone to care for your loved one while you either sought or maintained employment, you may qualify for the Child and Dependent Care Credit. Depending on your income, this credit may equal up to 35% of your qualifying expenses.

To claim the credit, the following conditions must be met:

- You must have earned income wages, salaries, tips, employee compensation, or net earnings from self-employment.
- Payments for care cannot be made to any person you claim as a dependent, or to your child under age 19.
- You must file as single, head of household, qualified widow(er) with a dependent child, or married filing jointly.

- The care must have been provided by a qualifying individual.
- The dependent must have lived with you for more than half of the year.

Remember to consult a local tax consultant for more help, information, and possible state-level deductions in your area.

Talk to Employers about Dependent Care FSAs

Consider utilizing a Dependent Care FSA (Flexible Spending Accounts) to help pay for medical/elder care expenses. These plans allow employees to contribute a portion of salary, before taxes, to accounts designated for health care expenses, including premiums and child/elder care expenses. Then employees are reimbursed from their accounts with tax free dollars for medical expenses and child/elder care expenses that can not be reimbursed. The funds must be used before the end of the plan year, or grace period, or else unused dollars are forfeited. If a caregiver has access to these plans, they should use them, but plan carefully so that contributions are not more than can be used in a year.

If an elderly parent lives with a participant and relies on that person for at least 50% of their support, then the Dependent Care FSA may be used for day care expenses. However, the care must be necessary to allow the participant to work and cannot be custodial nursing care. Also, if the participant is married, the care must be necessary because the spouse also works, is looking for work, or is a full-time student.

Common (Partial) Solutions to the Long-Term Care Crisis

Safety in the Home

How Can We Keep Seniors Safe in Their Own Home?

Keeping seniors safe includes making sure that the interior and exterior of the home is up-to-code, senior friendly, and accessible for those who are disabled. Interior safety includes modifications such as safety grab bars in the bathrooms, elevated toilet seats, and lower sink and vanity heights if needed. Kitchen cabinets can be lowered for easier accessibility. Doorways in older homes may be too narrow for walkers and wheelchairs and may need to be widened if possible. Levered door handles are a plus for everyone. Throw rugs are a bad idea in a senior's home; they contribute to falls more often than not. On the exterior of the home, there should be sturdy handrails wherever there are steps or uneven pavement. Senior friendly homes are now constructed on one level with no steps at the front door or garage entry. Many home builders are now specializing in senior living and are available for consultation. For a list of modifications, you can go to **www.AgingInPlace.com.**

Personal Emergency Response Systems

Personal emergency response systems (PERS) are another form of safety that should always be considered. A "PERS" is a system that can be set up very inexpensively in a senior's home. This is not just for "sick" people; these systems keep well people well. The senior wears a pendant around their neck, or a watch-style pendant, and has the system with them at all times inside and outside of the house. If they suffer a fall, stroke, illness, or any other event where they feel they might need assistance, all they have to do is access their system with the touch of a button.

Statistics

- A study by AC Nielson indicates among other things that seniors who have a personal emergency response system **stay at home an average of 6 years longer** than those who do not have a PERS. Also, most PERS have smoke detector options, keeping the home safe and protected from fire devastation.

- 58% of customers who have had a PERS for a year or more feel that their quality of life has improved.

- 87% of customers with a PERS think that this protection is important or a main factor in their decision to continue living at home.

- 95% of customers with a PERS feel protected at home.

- 80% feel that the comfort of living in their own home is important.

- 76% feel that being independent is important.

- **In a study of older adults, those living with a PERS reported significantly greater ability to go about their daily routine and were** *ten times* **less likely to require admission to a nursing home.**

- Medical research shows that falling down and being unable to get help is not an uncommon event. In fact, nearly **1/3** of all people over the age of 65 (and **half** of all people over 90) will fall each year. Of course, the older a senior gets, the more dangerous and debilitating falls can be, and they often mark the end of independent living.

- Research also tells us that 30% to 50% of elderly people fear falling—a fear that can cause them to lose confidence and restrict their normal range of healthy activities. The confidence and peace-of-mind that comes from a PERS helps to ease these anxieties as well as the feelings of isolation and depression caused by such worries.

Facts about Personal Emergency Response Systems

- **PERS are recommended by doctors, nurses and other professional caregivers.** They know even a minor fall or incident can have serious physical and psychological consequences if a senior cannot get help in a hurry.
- **A PERS is for independent living at home.** The alternative to getting a PERS is often assisted living, a nursing home, or 24-hour care.
- **A PERS is a good idea even if a senior does not live alone.** Accidents are unpredictable; a senior might need help when someone they live with is temporarily out of the house.
- **A PERS is easy to live with.** The personal help button is very small, simple to use, and will not interfere with a senior's activities in any way.
- **A PERS is for everyday living.** A PERS telephone also includes many other features that makes conversing with others more convenient, and can provide personalized reminders of important things to do.

Understanding Health Insurance and Medicare: *Does Medicare Pay for Long-Term Care?*

There is a common misconception about health insurance paying for the cost of long-term care; health insurance, including Medicare, Medicare Supplements, HMOs, private insurance through employers, and disability insurance, was never designed to pay for the cost of long-term care.

Medicare and Other Health Insurances

Medicare is a federal health insurance program for people 65 and older, certain people with disabilities, and those with ESRD (End Stage Renal Disease). It pays for much of your health care but not all of it; there are some costs you will have to pay yourself. **(www. medicare.gov)**

There are other kinds of health insurance that may help pay the costs that Medicare does not; Medicare Supplements (Medigap Policies) and long-term care insurance will pick up some of the costs that Medicare will not pay for.

Medicare was implemented in 1965. How many times has Medicare been over-hauled since 1965? NEVER. It was not designed to pay for care related to diseases or conditions such as Alzheimer's disease, Parkinson's, or MS. The average life expectancy was much lower in 1965 because medical technology was not as advanced. Medicare was designed for SHORT-TERM, acute care, and short-term, rehabilitative stays in a rehab or long-term care facility. Although Medicare Part D was added in 2004/2005 to help with the costs of prescription drugs, Medicare still does not pay for long-term care.

What Will Medicare Pay?

Medicare comes in four parts: Medicare Part A, Part B, Part C, and now Part D for prescription drugs.

Medicare Part A is Hospital Insurance.

Part A pays for inpatient hospital care, some skilled nursing-facility care, hospice care, and some home-health care. Most people get Medicare Part A automatically when they turn 65. There is usually no premium or monthly payment for Part A.

Medicare Part B is Medical Insurance.

Part B pays for doctor services, outpatient hospital care, and some other medical services that Part A does not pay for. Part B pays for these services and supplies when they are medically necessary. Part B has a premium that changes every year. The standard premium for Part B in 2023 is $164.90 per month, but may change depending on your reported gross income. (See table 5.1)

What Will Medicare A and B NOT Pay For?

Medicare carries some high deductibles. For instance, in 2023, during a hospital stay you will automatically have a $1,600 total deductible for days 1-60; on day 61 you are responsible for $400 (your deductible) per day through day 90; on day 91 you pay $800 per day (your deductible) through day 150, after which you pay all costs. This amounts to a substantial out-of-pocket expense for the Medicare recipient.

For a skilled nursing facility stay, Medicare pays for days 1-20; on day 21 you pay $200 through day 100. Beyond 101 days you are responsible for all costs.

Also, you will be responsible for 20% for most covered services under Part B, 50% for outpatient mental health treatment, and a co-pay for outpatient hospital services.[1]

> **Medicare was never designed to pay for long-term care. In other words, if you will be living in a nursing home or if you will need around-the-clock care at home, Medicare does not pay for these services. Medicare is for acute, short-term medical care and rehabilitative care only, otherwise called "skilled care."**

Defining Skilled Care vs. Custodial Care

Skilled care is defined as care that is prescribed by a physician and performed by a licensed health care professional, such as a nurse, physical therapist, or occupational therapist. Some examples of skilled care include: some wound care, IV antibiotics, or physical therapy immediately after a stroke.

Custodial care is another term for privately paid care. This type of care can be performed by home health aides or other unlicensed caregivers, such as family members. Some examples of custodial care include bathing, dressing, transferring from the bed to a chair, or toileting.

A Medicare Supplement policy will only cover some or all of the deductibles described above. This is a policy that you will have to

---

1   **2023 Medicare Costs** https://www.medicare.gov/Pubs/pdf/11579-medicare-costs.pdf

purchase separately. Medicare supplements will not pay for (custodial) long-term care costs; they simply cover the deductibles under Medicare and sometimes pay for a few extras.

Long-term care insurance will not cover Medicare deductibles like a Medicare Supplement policy will, but long-term care insurance will pay for all of the costs associated with long-term (custodial) nursing-home care, in-home care, assisted living, and adult day care.

Medicare Supplements

Medicare supplements, often referred to as Medigap plans, are purchased through private insurance companies to help fill the "gaps" that Medicare leaves behind. Medicare supplements pick up the co-pays and deductibles associated with standard Medicare. There are a number of standardized plans available. Each plan has a different set of benefits. Medicare supplements also do not cover the cost of long-term care; they simply pay deductibles and co-pays that Medicare does not.

Medicare Advantage Plans (Part C)

A Medicare Advantage plan is an "all in one" alternative to Original Medicare. These "bundled" plans include Part A, Part B, and usually Part D. In many cases, you will need to use doctors and specialists in the plan's network. Advantage plans may restrict the number of approved days for a hospital or skilled nursing rehab stay.

Private Insurance

Private health insurance through an employer or previous employer is essentially the same as a Part C plan as far as coverage. Standard health insurance, no matter how great the benefit, will ultimately fail to cover long-term care.

Disability Insurance

Disability insurance covers household expenses and is designed as income replacement. It will pay for things like groceries, rent, and utilities. This insurance was not designed to cover the added expense of long-term care.

Table 5.1

If your yearly income in 2021 (for what you pay in 2023) was:			
Filed individual tax return	Filed individual tax return	Filed married & separate tax return	You pay each month (in 2023)
$97,000 or less	$194,000 or less	$97,000 or less	$164.90
above $97,000 up to $123,000	above $194,000 up to $246,000	Not applicable	$230.80
above $123,000 up to $153,000	above $246,000 up to $306,000	Not applicable	$329.70
above $153,000 up to $183,000	above $306,000 up to $366,000	Not applicable	$428.60
above $183,000 and less than $500,000	above $366,000 and less than $750,000	above $97,000 and less than $403,000	$527.50
$500,000 or above	$750,000 or above	$403,000 or above	$560.50

Source: https://www.medicare.gov/Pubs/pdf/11579-medicare-costs.pdf

Understanding Medicaid

Medicaid Defined

Medicaid was established by federal law (Title XIX of the Social Security Act), and is administered by each state individually. Medicaid is a program for poor or "impoverished" people and people with high medical costs. Congress established Medicaid to provide a "safety net" for people who had no other way to pay for their health care or long-term care.

Medicaid is the long-term care payer of last resort for the frail elderly, persons with health problems, persons with mental retardation or mental illness, and those with physical or developmental disabilities.

Most long-term care and services, such as prescription drugs, eyeglasses and dental care, are provided at each state's discretion. When state money is scarce, these services may be the most vulnerable, not because of ill will on the part of the state decision makers, but because there may be nowhere else to cut state budgets.

Medicaid is a highly flawed program and is under-funded and over-burdened. States continue to make, and change, decisions about Medicaid that, among other things, will affect the amount of long-term care assistance available in each state, the eligibility, the criteria and number of persons eligible for that assistance, and the types of services that will be reimbursed.

The Deficit Reduction Act of 2005

President George W. Bush signed The Deficit Reduction Omnibus Reconciliation Act of 2005 on February 8, 2006. The new law tightens Medicaid's long-term care eligibility rules and allows for the nationwide expansion of the Long-Term Care (LTC) Partnership program.

This is great news for the long-term care insurance industry as it will encourage proper planning for future long-term care needs, and allow for the sale of Qualified State Long-Term Care Insurance policies (QSLTCI) under the new partnership program.

Changes to Medicaid Eligibility

The changes to Medicaid eligibility will make it harder for individuals to qualify for coverage. Such changes include:

- The look-back period for the transfer of assets is five years prior to applying for Medicaid coverage.
- Applicants will need to meet the required spend-down limits prior to the start of their penalty period (if they have a penalty period).
- Legislation will deny Medicaid coverage for nursing-home care to any applicant with home equity valued above $688,000 (up to $1,033,000 in some states).[2] This is indexed for inflation and can vary depending on where you live.

---

2   **Medicaid Eligibility: 2023 Income, Asset & Care Requirements for Nursing Homes & Long-Term Care** American Council on Aging https://www.medicaidplanningassistance.org/medicaid-eligibility/

Expansion of Partnership Long-Term Care Insurance Policies

The new law also includes the national expansion and availability of LTCI Partnership plans. Each individual state will have the opportunity to implement a Partnership program. Partnership policies help to protect state Medicaid budgets by requiring that the benefits of those qualifying insurance policies be paid before Medicaid benefits can be accessed. (The four existing partnership programs in CA, CT, IN, and NY will be grandfathered.)

The new Partnership policies allow consumers to protect a portion of their assets that they would typically need to spend down prior to qualifying for Medicaid coverage— ensuring that more of the funds accumulated for retirement will be protected.

Under the expansion of state Partnerships, states must have the same requirements for Partnership and Non-Partnership policies. The objective, as states elect to participate, is to have uniform requirements. Essentially, any tax-qualified LTCI policy approved by a state insurance department that meets the requirements of the federal Partnership program would qualify for asset protection, on a dollar-for-dollar basis, up to the policy maximum.

Assets that must be spent down in order to qualify for Medicaid include:

- cash
- checking/saving accounts
- CDs
- savings bonds
- investment accounts/mutual funds/stocks
- IRA's and other retirement accounts
- vacation homes and investment properties
- second car
- certain real estate or personal property not in use

Assets that a person can keep for purposes of qualifying for Medicaid include: [3]

- a home (a principal residence with equity under the requirements for your state)
- household goods
- personal effects
- automobile—one per person
- life insurance (no more than $1,500 in cash surrender value)
- *irrevocable* prepaid burial plan.
- property essential to the individual's self support (perhaps a small business)
- income producing property—other than cash, with some restrictions (like farmed land or rental)

Reverse Mortgages and Medicaid

Reverse mortgages do not affect Medicare (including Medicare Part D) or Social Security income. However, the proceeds from a reverse mortgage CAN affect local income-based programs in your area, and the big one—Medicaid.

The first thing to remember is that aging adults should answer a lot of questions regarding their plans for the cash flow or lump sum received from a reverse mortgage:

- Are they already in poor health?
- Do they intend to "gift" the money away to relatives?
- Are they using the money to pay for in-home care?
- Do they have long-term care insurance already?
- Are they planning on applying for Medicaid anytime soon?

---

3   Medicaid's Community Spouse Resource Allowance (CSRA): Calculations & Limits American Council on Aging https://www.medicaidplanningassistance.org/community-spouse-resource-allowance/#countable

If the answer to any of these questions is yes, they would be well advised to consult a local elder law attorney (**www.naela.org**). Keep in mind that most elder law attorneys need education about reverse mortgages. It is always a good idea to check with an elder law attorney who understands all aspects of Reverse Mortgages and Medicaid. An aging adult may also be wise to consider having a son, daughter or other advocate accompany them when consulting an attorney.

The bottom line is that if someone needs to be on Medicaid soon, or already there, then "gifting" and additional cash flow in their checking accounts or savings accounts can knock them out of eligibility quickly!

If your family member is thinking about taking the "lump sum" option available through a reverse mortgage, you might ask them to consider leaving the money in the line of credit. When they make a withdrawal from the line of credit (to pay bills, buy a new appliance, fix the air conditioner or heater) they must spend that money the same month that the withdrawal from the line of credit hits their checking account. Even then, they need to keep receipts for service and goods purchased to prove that they didn't give the money away.

If that extra cash flow sits in their checking or savings account for more than 30 days, it could knock them out of eligibility.

If a senior decides that they want to receive the monthly check to increase their cash flow, they should make sure that they need the money every month to pay bills. If that checking account starts adding up, or if they are above the allowed amount of income because of the additional cash flow, they may be getting into trouble.

Do not assume that your family member knows the rules because the rules are complicated and change regularly. Talk to someone who knows and studies these laws all of the time.

Prenuptial Agreements

For second marriages, this information is particularly important.

"What's mine is mine, what's his is his. They won't touch MY money for HIS long-term care, right?"

Yes, they will. Prenuptial agreements hold no weight when it comes to Medicaid. When two people are married, their assets become marital property. So even if Nancy has $1 million dollars, and Robert has $5,000 dollars, it does not really matter. If one of them needs care, and they have no long-term care insurance, they will have to go through the spend-down process considering both of their combined assets.

Mandatory Estate Recovery

In August, 1993, the federal government enacted a new law: the state must seek recovery of Medicaid expenditures from the estate of a deceased individual who was 55 or older when he or she received assistance.

This means that when the person on Medicaid dies, the state will collect the amount they spent on that person's care from the remaining estate. The state must include all real estate, personal property, and other assets included within an estate under the state's probate law. The state may also include other property in which the individual had an interest at the time of death. If the deceased Medicaid recipient has a spouse still living in the home (community spouse), that spouse can usually continue living in the home until his or her death, before the state will seek recovery. A Medicaid lien is usually placed on the property of the Medicaid recipient.

If a child caregiver has lived with mom or dad for two years or more, and if mom or dad would not have been able to live on their own but for child living with them, the house may be transferred or given to the child with no Medicaid penalty.

Transferring Assets

"I'll Just Give It All Away!"

When a person applies for Medicaid to pay for medical care, federal law requires the state to consider recent transfers of assets and monetary gifts. If a person or his or her spouse has transferred assets for less than fair market value in the 60 months (5 years) prior to applying for Medicaid, or at any time after applying, the applicant will be considered "ineligible" for a period of time based on the amount transferred. In the case of assets transferred to a "trust," the look-back period is the same—60 months. The look-back period means that the state can go back 5 years and see if any transfers have been made and add them (based on a specific calculation) to the ineligibility period.

Divorce

If Robert and Nancy had given $120,000 to their wonderful daughter, Susan, for safe keeping 6 years prior to Robert's stroke, Robert would almost immediately be eligible for Medicaid.

But what if Susan's husband, Scott, decided that he wanted a divorce? Technically, in most states that money would be considered marital property and would be divided in half, leaving Susan with only $60,000 of her parent's money.

Lawsuits

Susan has her parent's $120,000 in a bank account in her and her husband's names. Husband Scott is in a car accident, and the other party sues Scott for damages beyond what his insurance company will pay. The plaintiff's lawyer sees $120,000 sitting in their account. If he wins the case, they may lose it all.

Financial Aid

Susan and Scott have a daughter who will be 18 in a few months and is looking forward to going away to college. The family applies for financial aid, but because they have Susan's parent's $120,000 in their account, their daughter does not qualify for financial aid.

Buying Toys

Susan and Scott have always been fairly responsible, but have decided that they need that new boat. Susan's parents, Robert and Nancy, will not know if they borrow just $20,000. The kids will be sure to pay it back…eventually.

Comprehensive Long-Term Care Solutions Using Private Pay Strategies

Traditional Long-Term Care Insurance and the Partnership Plan

How Much Does Long-Term Care Insurance Cost?

Of course, the cost of long-term care insurance depends on many different choices and options. The more bells and whistles, the more costly the plan. The most important thing to remember is that long-term care insurance premiums will NEVER cost as much as a few months in a nursing home without the insurance (see Chapter 1). The problem for most people is that long-term care insurance premiums may seem unaffordable, even though they are the most cost effective way to plan ahead.

Recognizing this, the federal government introduced the LTC Partnership Program.

The Partnership Program couples the purchase of long-term care insurance with eligibility for Medicaid coverage for LTC services. With the purchase of a Partnership policy, a consumer can become eligible for Medicaid coverage after using the insurance benefits without having to exhaust his or her own assets to qualify for such coverage. Assets equal to the amount expended by the insurance policy are not considered countable assets for purposes of Medicaid eligibility and are exempt from the Medicaid estate recovery provisions. (One significant caveat; those with home equity exceeding $688,000 are not eligible for Medicaid even with the Partnership policy although states may increase that ceiling to $1,033,000.)

Traditional Long-Term Care Insurance

Traditional long-term care insurance used to be viewed as "nursing-home insurance" because most policies from 15 years ago only offered that one option. Today that is hardly the case; long-term care insurance now covers adult day care, in-home care, assisted living, and nursing-home care. These policies are considered comprehensive in nature. Now we refer to long-term care insurance as "lifestyle insurance."

Who Cannot Get Long-Term Care Insurance?

Underwriting Explained

When you apply for a long-term care insurance plan, you must go through underwriting. Underwriting means that the company will check your medical records to determine what medical problems you may currently have or have had in the past. They want to know your overall health history. If you have been diagnosed with short-term memory loss, Alzheimer's disease, Parkinson's disease, Multiple Sclerosis, Lou Gehrig's disease, or if you have had a stroke with permanent physical impairment, you may not qualify. People who have survived cancer and are treatment free for a certain length of time can often qualify. Each insurance company has their own underwriting guidelines. It is best to talk to your agent or call the company directly with any specific questions about health issues. Height and weight are also a consideration when applying. Sometimes the insurance company will send a registered nurse to the home to ask a few questions and take some more medical history, or they may just call on the phone for a brief interview.

Qualifying to USE the Benefits of a Long-Term Care Insurance Plan

Activities of Daily Living

When it is time to use your tax-qualified long-term care insurance plan (taxes to be discussed in a later chapter), the insured person must need help or substantial assistance with 2 out of 6 activities of daily living for a period of 90 days or greater. This need for care must be certified by a licensed healthcare practitioner such as a nurse or physician.

These activities of daily living include:

1. bathing
2. dressing
3. eating
4. toileting
5. continence
6. transferring (i.e. moving from the bed to a chair)

Or the insured must have a cognitive impairment like Alzheimer's disease or dementia. A cognitive impairment means that although a person may be physically able to perform all of the activities listed above, they cannot remember or rationalize how to do those activities. One example would be bathing; sometimes people with dementia are physically able to take a bath, but cannot remember to do so, cannot remember why this is important, or perhaps when getting dressed, they put on 5 shirts instead of one.

Comprehensive vs. Facility-Only Plans

Comprehensive Plans

A comprehensive plan covers all aspects of long-term care: in-home care, adult day care, assisted living, and nursing-home care. These plans are designed to help people stay at home longer and also to assist them with transitions to other levels of care as needed. Most consumers want to stay at home for as long as possible. A comprehensive plan will satisfy that desire.

Facility-Only Coverage

Facility-only plans are still available on the market today. Facility-only plans pay for just that, facility care only. Usually this includes assisted living and nursing-home care. A facility only plan makes the most sense for folks who do not have a large network of family and friends around them, and for people who know that this may be their only option in the future. Facility-only plans are less costly than comprehensive plans but, again, offer payment only for nursing-home and assisted- living care. The insured person cannot live at home and use the benefits of a facility-only plan.

Benefit Period

The benefit period is the length of time during which the policy will actually pay for care. There are many different benefit periods available including 2 years, 3 years, 4 years, 5 years, 7 years, 10 years, and unlimited lifetime coverage. When purchasing long-term care insurance, keep in mind that premiums are paid for potentially the next 20 years (or until the policy holder needs care), but the plan will only last about as long as the benefit period originally selected.

People often ask, "How do I know which benefit period to choose?" "How do I know how long I might need care?"

Obviously there is no way to really determine how long a person might need care. However, the best advice for each individual is to take a look at their own personal health history and their family history; if there is a history of chronic disease such as Alzheimer's, Parkinson's, MS, or Lou Gehrig's disease, it might be worthwhile to consider a longer benefit period.

The average length of stay in a nursing home is about 2.8 years; the average care-giving time at home is about 4.1 years.

Daily Benefit Amount

The daily benefit amount is the maximum amount a plan will pay on a daily or weekly basis. Some policies now pay based on a weekly or monthly maximum. In this case, it is important to know the average cost of care in the local area. The current national average cost of a semi-private nursing home bed is around $260 per day or $7,908 per month. Consider the cost of care in the area where you live and the cost of care in an area where you might retire, and plan accordingly.

A semi-private room in a nursing home means that two people share a room. A private room in a nursing home means that the room is for one person only. A private room will cost significantly more than a semi-private room. Be sure to factor in the extra cost if a private room is expected.

For some people the insurance policy's daily benefit amount does not need to cover the entire cost of care. If there is some Social Security income or pension income that can pick up a portion of the long-term care costs, then perhaps some premium can be saved by having a lower daily benefit amount.

Keep in mind however, that $260/day covers the cost of room and board only, not the added cost of the care needed, prescription drugs, supplies such as adult incontinence protection, and other necessities. The additional expense of these items can add as much as 20% to 50% per day on to the cost of a nursing home bed.

Elimination Period

The elimination period is similar to a deductible or a waiting period. This is the length of time a person must wait before their plan will begin to pay. Elimination periods vary from company to company and plan to plan. The elimination period choices include 0 days, 30 days, 60 days, 90 days, 100 days, and 180 days. Some plans will offer to waive the elimination period for home care under certain circumstances, and some offer riders that will eliminate or decrease waiting periods. Be aware that some elimination periods are based on dates of service. Therefore, if only one day of home care is needed per week and the elimination period is 30 days, it could take as much as 30 weeks to satisfy that elimination period. On the other hand, many companies today will allow one day of home care to count as 7 days toward the elimination period. This is a nice strategy and is useful in encouraging people to stay home longer.

The shorter the elimination period, the more expensive the premium.

Inflation Protection Options

The average cost of health care rises anywhere from 4% to 7% per year. Therefore $260 per day today won't be enough coverage 10 years from now when the cost is actually around $350 per day, so it is important to build in some protection against the cost of inflation.

There are typically three types of inflation protection that are available. One is compound inflation protection, which provides an automatic increase in benefits every year (usually at 5%) with no corresponding increase in premium. This is the most expensive inflation protection, but is well worth the investment. For consumers who buy long-term care insurance at younger ages, for example anyone under age 70, compound inflation protection offers the most complete coverage.

Simple inflation protection is also usually at 5% per year but is not compounded. This inflation protection will grow at a slower rate than compound inflation protection and is often recommended for folks over age 70. There is no corresponding increase in premium.

Finally, there is a future purchase option offered on some plans. This option allows the consumer to decide at a later time whether they would like to buy a greater daily benefit amount to catch up with the current cost of care. If no extra benefit is purchased, the daily benefit amount remains the same and the premium does not increase. If extra benefit is purchased, the premium increases to the new benefit level. No further underwriting is required for future purchase option benefit increases.

Care Coordination Benefits

Some plans will offer care coordination as a built-in benefit. Care coordination is a valuable service for both the person receiving care and for the other family members involved. Long-term care insurers recognize that sometimes it is difficult for a senior or a family member to know which services in their local area might be most appropriate and give the best quality care available. Care coordinators are licensed professionals such as Registered Nurses and Licensed Social Workers who have experience in home health and coordinating care for seniors in their local areas. Some companies will require the plan member to use a care coordinator designated by the insurer. Other companies will allow a family to choose that care coordinator. They will allot a certain amount of money to be used toward a comprehensive in-home evaluation and plan of care. Either way, this service is invaluable and takes the fear and confusion out of selecting a long-term care provider. Care coordinators are not "gatekeepers"; they are simply healthcare professionals who know the system and the local resources. They are there for guidance and assistance along the way.

Home Care and Community Care Benefits

Home and Community Care includes services provided by a licensed home health agency. This can include services from a Registered Nurse, Licensed Practical Nurse, Physical Therapist, Occupational Therapist, Nurse's Aide, homemaker services (non-medical services), at-home hospice care, and adult day care. Some plans with enhanced home care provisions, or riders, will also allow (with authorization) a friend or family member to provide care. That family member will be reimbursed for their time and expense. A family member usually cannot be someone who normally lives in the same home as the person going on claim. In other words, most long-term care insurance companies do not want to pay a spouse to be the sole caregiver.

Facility Care

Facility care most often refers to care received in a nursing home, hospice facility, or assisted-living facility. The plan will usually cover room and board, nursing care, maintenance or personal care, and hospice care in that facility. Most plans will also offer a bed reservation benefit, meaning that if a person leaves the facility for the weekend, or is hospitalized, the insurer will pay for that amount of time to hold the bed even though the insured is not in the facility. Most bed reservation benefits last about 30 days per policy year.

Respite Care Benefits

Respite care, simply defined, is a break for the caregiver. For example, if daughter Susan is caring for her father, she may need a break from time to time. If she decides to take a long weekend and go on vacation, a formal caregiver can be hired to take her place.

Respite care can be received in a nursing home or adult day care, in-home, or in a hospice facility. The insurer will pay the maximum daily benefit for up to 21 days per year on average. The insured does not have to meet the elimination period in order to use respite care benefits.

Alternate Plan of Care

"Alternate plan of care" usually refers to services that are not already clearly defined in the plan. Most alternate plans of care must be approved by the insurer, but would include services designed to enhance quality of life or designed to keep a person safe in their home for a longer period of time. Examples include a personal emergency service, like LifeLine, or perhaps a wheelchair ramp that would enhance accessibility to the insured's home.

Caregiver Training

Caregiver training is useful when an informal caregiver needs to learn how to bathe, transfer, feed, or dress someone receiving long-term care. A licensed or formally trained professional will provide the training to the informal caregiver. This ensures that the care being received is quality care and is provided in a safe and efficient manner. This training will be paid for by the plan.

Bells and Whistles (The Riders)

Riders can be purchased in addition to the standard long-term care insurance plan and offer flexibility in plan design.

Shared Benefits

Some plans will allow spouses and families to share benefits. One example would be the sharing of a benefit between husband and wife. In this case, the husband and wife choose an 8-year plan.

If he needs to use 6 years of the plan, she will have 2 years left to use when she needs long-term care. A shared benefit plan might be recommended to a couple who have been married for many years and who are roughly the same age.

Survivorship

Survivorship typically means that if both spouses are insured by the same company with no claim having been made in 7 to 10 years, and one spouse passes away, the other spouse's plan will be paid up in full. There will be no further premium due for the surviving spouse and coverage will continue.

Return of Premium

Return of premium takes away the fear: "If I don't use it, I'll lose it!" This simply means that if a claim has never been made and the insured person passes away, the premium paid will be returned to the surviving heirs. There are several variations on the theme and each company handles return of premium differently. Pay close attention to contract language in the policy.

Waiver of Premium

In many cases, waiver of premium is a built-in feature of a long-term care insurance plan, but in some cases it can be purchased as an extra rider. Waiver of premium means that when the insured files a claim and begins using their benefits, they no longer pay premiums to the insurance company. Usually, waiver of premium goes into effect after the elimination period has been satisfied.

Indemnity

The typical long-term care insurance plan is a reimbursement plan, meaning that the insurance company reimburses the care providers after a claim has been submitted. However, some plans now offer an indemnity situation. This type of plan will pay the insured the daily or monthly benefit, and it is up to the insured to pay the care providers. This type of plan is more flexible and usually more expensive. However, the insured has more options when choosing a care provider. For instance, instead of using a local home health agency, the insured person may want to pay a son or daughter to care for them. Indemnity plans require that the insured, or their legal representative, makes good choices about care and is able to use the money wisely.

Important Consideration When Choosing a Long-Term Care Plan

Ratings

The financial ratings of a company are important when considering purchasing a long-term care insurance plan. The recommendation is to choose a company with an AM BEST rating of A+ or better.

Assets

Assets of the insurance company should be in the BILLIONS.

Discounts

Some long-term care insurers will allow for group discounts through employers, or "affinity" group discounts through a local organization. Senior clubs and organizations all across America offer discounts from 5% to 10% on long-term care insurance. Not all companies permit these types of discounts; however, there are some discounts that almost all long-term care insurers include in their plans. These include spousal (or partner) discounts and good health discounts. Spousal discounts are applied when a couple applies for the insurance together. Discounts of this kind range anywhere from 30 to 50%. Good health discounts are given when the applicant is in excellent health. Each company has its own underwriting guidelines for health discounts. These will range from 10% to 15%.

Tax Considerations

Currently, there are some tax advantages regarding tax qualified long-term care insurance plans. At the federal level, premiums for long-term care insurance fall into the "medical expense" category, so if the premium (or the premium plus other medical expenses) is over 7.5% of the adjusted gross income, part of that premium is tax deductible. Taxpayers must be able to itemize in order to take advantage of the federal deduction. It is important to talk to a tax advisor or accountant for that information as it changes every year.

Business owners, especially those with C-Corporations, can deduct the full cost of long-term care insurance protection for themselves and designated individuals, including spouses.

On the state level, 26 states offer some form of deduction or tax credit for long-term care insurance premiums. In the state of Missouri, for example, premiums are 100% tax deductible. This is an "above the line" deduction so there is no need to itemize to take advantage of the savings. Again, it is important to see an accountant or tax advisor for tax advantages state by state.

Tax Qualified Plans vs. Non-Tax Qualified Plans

To make matters a little more complicated, there are two types of standard long-term care insurance plans available. Tax qualified plans follow the federal HIPAA law (Health Insurance Portability and Accountability Act). For these plans, the insured must need assistance with 2 out of 6 activities of daily living, for a period of 90 days or greater, in order to qualify to use their benefits. This law protects consumers in several ways. It insures that long-term care insurance is truly designed for long-term care—greater than 90 days. The benefits received are not considered taxable income. Tax qualified plans are guaranteed renewable. This means that your coverage can never be canceled as long as you pay your premiums.

Non-tax qualified plans allow the consumer to access benefits more quickly. With these plans, the insured only needs to prove that they require assistance with 1 out of 5 activities of daily living, with an attending physician's statement. Non-tax qualified plans are usually a bit more expensive than tax qualified plans. The jury is still out on whether or not the benefits are taxable as income. In the insurance world, there is a great debate on the pros and cons of each plan.

Payment Options for Long-Term Care Insurance

Annual Premium Payment

"Annual premium payment" means that the insured person will pay premiums yearly for a lifetime or until they use their long-term care insurance. Payments can also be made monthly, quarterly, or semi-annually. Like auto or homeowners insurance, if payments are made on a monthly, quarterly, or semi-annual basis, there is usually an additional fee. Once the insured has a claim approved, most policies will waive the premium after the elimination period has been satisfied.

10-Pay

The 10-pay option allows the insured to pay a higher premium for a shorter period of time—10 years. After 10 years of premium payment, no further premiums are due.

Pay to 65

Some plans offer the option for the insured person to pay premiums until they are 65. At age 65, no further premium is due. This is a nice option because at retirement age, income may be significantly less than that of working-age adults.

Lump-Sum (One-Time) Payment

Some consumers have the option to pay a one-time, lump-sum premium. This means that no further premium is ever due. Many business owners find this option attractive for the tax deduction in the year that they purchase the policy. Asset-based, long-term care insurance is also a one-time payment.

Annuity-Based Long-Term Care and the Pension Protection Act of 2006

On August 17, 2006, the President signed into law The Pension Protection Act of 2006 (the "Act"). Individuals owning annuity contracts can now have long-term care riders with special tax advantages. The Act allows the cash value of annuity contracts to be used to pay premiums on long-term care contracts. The payment of premiums in this manner will reduce the cost basis of the annuity contract. In addition, the Act allows annuity contracts without long-term care riders to be exchanged for contracts with such a rider in a tax-free transfer under Section 1035 of the Internal Revenue Code of 1986, as amended ("IRC"). This provision may prove beneficial to individuals who own annuities with a low cost basis and those who are not in the best of health. The cash value of the annuity can be used to purchase long-term care insurance. This provision is effective for exchanges which take place after 2009. Since COVID-19 there has been a move by some insurance companies to offer annuities that conform to the pension protection act annuities on a guaranteed issue basis. This may be particularly helpful if you already have a loved one who is receiving care or was just recently diagnosed with one of over 70 types of dementia.

An example of how an annuity-based long-term care plan could help someone is illustrated in Exhibit 8.1. For this example, we will call our client Bob, age 70, and recently widowed. His children lived out of town and they were very concerned about what would happen if dad needed some additional care in the future. Since Bob had some health concerns and was recently diagnosed with diabetes, along with a history of heart disease, he was not a good candidate for traditional long-term care insurance. However, by taking advantage of an annuity based long-term care strategy that takes advantage of the Pension Protection Act, Bob could likely be insured. By taking his $140,000 fixed annuity with a cost basis of only 40,000 (i.e. the amount he actually deposited) and using the IRS 1035 tax-free exchange from his existing fixed annuity to a new annuity that complied with the rules laid out in the Pension Protection Act, Bob's $140,000 fixed annuity could continue to earn interest. However, if he needed long-term care to pay for home care, assisted living, or skilled care he now had a long-term care benefit pool equal to $420,000. (See exhibit 8.1.)*

Exhibit 8.1

Bob (70) Current Situation

$300,000
Money
Market

$37,000
Checking

$140,000
Fixed
Annuity

$240,000
Home

(cost basis $40,000)

- recently widowed
- adult children live out of town
- health concerns—insulin diabetes with history of heart disease

Bob (70) Proposed

$140,000
Fixed
Annuity

Combo LTC Annuity

$420,000
LTC Pool

Hypothetically, by repositioning his fixed annuity...

- Bob retains his $140,000 in cash value plus an additional $280,000 for a total of $420,000 for long-term care.
- His benefits may be used for home care, assisted living, and skilled care.
- He pays no annual premiums.
- As his annuity grows, so does his LTC!
  (Assuming he does not use his LTC benefit.)

Examples are hypothetical. Results are not guaranteed. Consult a tax or financial professional.

Asset-Based Long-Term Care Strategy

Legacy assets are those assets in a retiree's portfolio that do not support their lifestyle but are available in case of some serious emergency (rainy day money!). These assets, if (hopefully) never needed, will probably pass to the clients' children, church, or charity after they die. The one most significant risk to those assets is the need to pay for long-term care.

Many people in this situation resist the idea of conventional long-term care insurance, not wanting to admit that they might need it, and taking the position that they can pay for any care out of pocket. They are choosing to "self insure." For these individuals, the ideal planning approach would be to "invest" some of their legacy assets in such a way that the assets can be worth as much as possible whenever they may be needed to pay for care, in the home, assisted-living facility, or nursing home. If not needed, the money would then pass to the intended heirs, with no "use it, or lose it" issues as with conventional long-term care insurance.

To employ this strategy, money is transferred from its current location (bank account, fixed annuity, etc.) into a specially-designed life insurance policy with riders that prepay the death benefit, and additionally to reimburse the insured for the incurred costs of long-term care. Depending on age, sex and health status, the money paid into one of these policies may be worth twice as much if the insured dies without ever needing to use it. Also, if needed for convalescent care, the insured can receive up to five times the amount of benefits deposited into the contract. Any money not used for that purpose would then pass to the heirs at death (See Exhibit 10.1).*

While invested in the insurance policy, the client's money is safe and available for any other reason at any time. There is usually a money-back guarantee that assures that the policyholder will always have access to the funds. Rather than a typical "purchase" of insurance, the transaction is more like "moving money from one account to another"—a cash value account that provides the same "savings" features as the bank, bond, or annuity from which it came.

Because the actual cost of long-term care is so great (potentially $60,000 to $100,000 per year or more) and the average need exceeds 2 years, these policies are usually purchased with a rider that extends the long-term care benefits after the death benefit has been exhausted. These riders effectively double or triple the benefit so that in the example (See Exhibit 10.1), a $50,000 premium deposit can provide as much as $250,000 in total long-term care benefits, providing as much as six years worth of protection.

This approach is ideal for those individuals who reject the idea of purchasing conventional, annual-premium long-term care insurance policies and take the position that if they ever need long-term convalescent care, they will pay for it using their own assets.

For individuals who do not, for whatever reason, want to own any life insurance, there is an alternative. Since the objective is to leverage up the individual's assets if long-term care is needed, some insurance companies are now offering fixed index annuities with guaranteed income riders that double should the individual enter a nursing home (See Exhibit 10.2).

* Not all products are available in all states.

Exhibit 10.1

Mary's Hypothetical Situation

Proposed Strategy

- It provides LTC by repositioning assets.
- Mary can choose where to receive care with income tax-free LTC benefits.
- Income tax-free death benefit for children if she does not need long-term care.
- 100% of the premium is returned (within the time frame and conditions allowed in the policy) if Mary changes her mind or finds a better solution.
- LTC benefits are guaranteed without worries of future premium increases.

    Note: The death benefit on these policies typically declines dollar for dollar based on the amount of LTC benefit needed. If Mary needs a $20,000 LTC withdrawal, her death benefit would be reduced by $20,000 to $80,000.

Mary (65) **Proposed Asset-Preservation Strategy Combo Life & LTC**
(65-year-old female non-smoker in good health)

Premium $50,000	Death Benefit $98,334	Long-Term Care Benefit $274,764
Premium-Back Guarantee	*Income Tax-Free*	*Choices on Where to Receive the Care*

Source: Total Living Coverage, Genworth Insurance Company

Examples are hypothetical. Results are not guaranteed. Consult a tax or financial professional.

Finally, of all the contingencies faced in retirement, long-term care is probably the most difficult and perhaps the most costly, financially as well as emotionally. These asset-based long-term care strategies allow wise consumers to

1. Manage their money
2. Provide significantly for such a possibility without committing large annual insurance premiums to something they sincerely hope will never be needed.

Since the money to do this must reside somewhere, these asset-based long-term care products provide a safe and financially rewarding option.

Exhibit 10.2

Income Preferred Series Calculator

Year Issue	Attained Age	Income Base	Withdrawal Percentage	Withdrawal Payment	Enhanced Withdrawal Payment
0	75	$354,000	n/a	n/a	n/a
1	76	$354,000	5.90%	$20,886	n/a
2	77	$354,000	6.00%	$21,240	n/a
3	78	$362,385	6.00%	$21,743	$43,486
4	79	$385,940	6.00%	$23,156	$46,313
5	80	$411,026	6.00%	$24,662	$49,323
6	81	$437,743	6.00%	$26,265	$52,529
7	82	$466,196	6.00%	$27,972	$55,944
8	83	$496,499	6.00%	$29,790	$59,580
9	84	$528,771	6.00%	$31,726	$63,453
10	85	$563,141	6.00%	$33,788	$67,577
11	86	$599,745	6.00%	$35,985	$71,969
12	87	$638,729	6.00%	$38,324	$76,647
13	88	$680,246	6.00%	$40,815	$81,630
14	89	$724,462	6.00%	$43,468	$86,935
15	90	$771,552	6.00%	$46,293	$92,586
16	91	$821,703	6.00%	$49,302	$98,604
17	92	$875,114	6.00%	$52,507	$105,014
18	93	$931,996	6.00%	$55,920	$111,840
19	94	$992,576	6.00%	$59,555	$119,109
20	95	$1,057,094	6.00%	$63,426	$126,851

* Not all products are available in all states.

Product:
Fixed Index Annuity*

Initial Premium:
$300,000 (includes any applicable bonus)

Issue Age: 75
Years to Defer: 10
Withdrawal Attained Age: 85

Joint Annuitant: No
Mode of Withdrawal: Annual

The printouts and results displayed by this calculator are approved for consumer use. Please note the actual use and inputting of values are only for appointed LTC producers. The assumptions used in this illustration are guaranteed based on the assumptions you provide in the calculation. The use of alternative premium, age, product, deferral years, and joint life assumptions may produce significantly different results.

Long-Term Care Strategy Using IRA Money

Most people use their IRA to supplement retirement. Some wait to take distributions on their IRA's until they turn 72, at which point it is mandatory to take RMDs (required minimum distributions). However, others have chosen to take a portion of their IRA and fund an IRA-based annuity (called a trustee-to-trustee transfer), which they subsequently use to fund a 20-pay life insurance plan with long-term care features. This type of IRA-based long-term care policy is unique in the sense that it starts out as an IRA annuity policy, also known as a tax qualified annuity, and then over a twenty year period makes equal distribution internally to the insurance carrier and funds the life insurance. The owner of the IRA annuity will receive a 1099R every year for 20 years (the IRS tax form that reports the taxable amount of an IRA distribution) on the amount of the IRA annuity that is moved annually to fund the life insurance policy.

Let's look at an example. We will use Tim, age 60, recently widowed, and retired. While he feels very secure about his retirement income, his main concern is long-term care and how to pay for it. Like many people his age, he is what we call "qualified money rich ... non-qualified poor." In other words, Tim has a lot more

Exhibit 11.1

Tim (60)

Current Situation

$500,000
IRA

**No Long-Term
Care Insurance**

Tim (60)

Proposed

$343,000
IRA
Maintain

*Tax-Free
Transfer*

$157,000
IRA

*If LTC is
Not Needed*

$237,000
Death
Benefit*

If Long-Term Care is Needed
Lifetime Long-Term Care Monthly Benefit – $5,367
*Can Pay For: Home Health • Assisted Living • Adult Day Care
• Nursing Home*

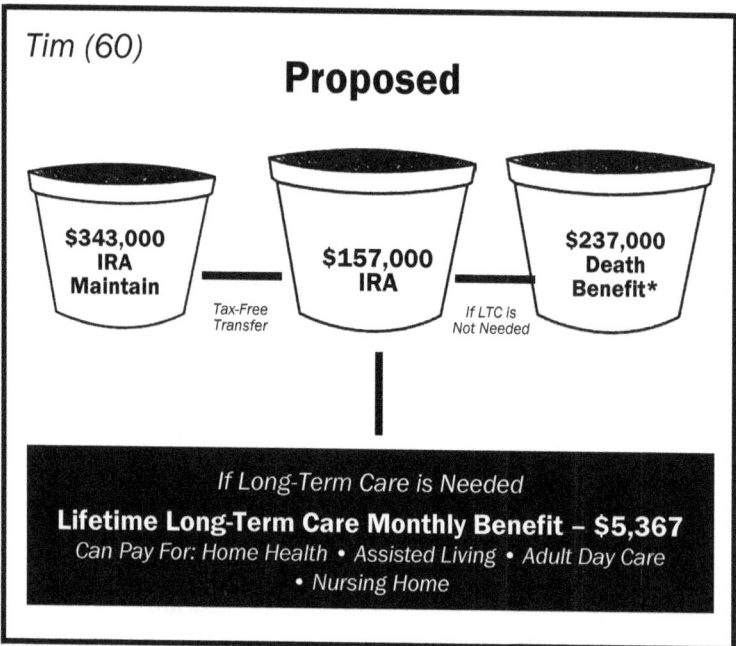

* Not all products are available in all states.

Examples are hypothetical. Results are not guaranteed. Consult a tax or financial professional.

IRA type money (before tax) than he does after tax money. By taking advantage of a tax-free trustee to trustee transfer, Tim is able to reposition $157,000 of his $500,000 IRA account into an IRA-based annuity. This IRA annuity will fund a life policy that can provide a pool of long-term money should he need it in the future. By doing this, he will create a death benefit in the amount of $237,000 that will be paid to his children upon his death. More important than the death benefit is that should Tim ever need long-term care, this policy will provide a monthly benefit of $9,488 that can be used to pay for home healthcare, assisted living, adult day care or even skilled nursing-home care (See Exhibit 11.1).

Let's look at another example. This example will show the impact of using an IRA-based long-term policy for a married couple. Both Beth, age 60, and her husband Bob, age 65, are concerned about long-term care but up to this point have been scared away from purchasing traditional stand-alone long-term care policies due to the requirement that annual premiums have to be paid. While they do not need additional income from Bob's IRA, they would like to help their children avoid paying taxes on the IRA account when both Bob and Beth have passed away. In the case of a married couple, this is when the taxes on an IRA are due. By taking advantage of a tax-free, trustee to trustee transfer, Bob decides to transfer $240,000 from his IRA into an IRA annuity that will fund a 10 year pay life insurance policy. Bob will receive a 1099-R annually for the IRA dollar amount that is internally moved from his IRA annuity to the life insurance policy. Beth is included, along with Bob as an insured on the life policy so that upon the death of Bob and Beth, their children will receive a death benefit in the amount of $290,000. The life insurance portion of this program is referred to as a second-to-die life insurance policy. More importantly, by making this IRA transfer they have secured $8,708 of monthly long-term care benefit for both of them! This monthly long-term care benefit can be used to pay for home healthcare, assisted living, adult day care, or even skilled nursing care. (see exhibit 11.2)

Exhibit 11.2

Beth (60) Bob (65)

Long-Term Care Strategy for Couples Using IRA

$540,000 IRA

$145,000 Checking/ Savings

$3,800/mo Pension/ Social Security

- They are concerned about long-term care.
- They have been scared away from traditional LTC insurance premiums.
- They would like to avoid taxes on IRA at 2nd death.

Beth (60) Bob (65)

Beth and Bob's Solution

IRA Trustee-to- Trustee Transfer $240,000

By Transitioning a Portion of His IRA

Benefits for LTC or 2nd Death Benefit* $290,000

- $9,049 monthly benefit for life of both
- covers home health, assisted living, and skilled care
- Bob receives a 1099 on his RMD

* Not all products are available in all states.

Examples are hypothetical. Results are not guaranteed. Consult a tax or financial professional.

Long-Term Care Solutions Using Government Benefits and Legal Strategies

Legal Documents Needed for Long-Term Care Planning

Legal Matters

One of the most important things to set in motion before care is required is the legal paperwork! A durable power of attorney for health care and a financial power of attorney are essential, along with an advanced directive or living will.

Elder law attorneys can help with:

- trusts
- wills
- durable powers of attorney
- Medicaid and VA benefits
- advanced medical directives
- other important legal issues and documents

What is a "Power of Attorney"?

A power of attorney (POA) is a document whereby one person (called the "principal") authorizes another individual or entity (called an "agent" or "attorney-in-fact") to act on behalf of the principal. The most common uses for a POA are financial transactions and health care decisions. Most states have one set of laws governing financial POAs and a second set of laws governing POAs for health care decisions. Therefore, it is the common and recommended practice not to mix the two purposes into one document. An individual desiring to have a POA covering both financial and medical situations should prepare two separate POAs, one dealing with financial issues and the second dealing with medical issues.

When Should I Have a Financial Power of Attorney?

Persons with physical handicaps or limitations often set up financial POAs, with a family member as the agent, to allow the family member to do such routine matters as making withdrawals from the principal's bank account. It would otherwise be a burden for the principal with physical limitations to make the short trips personally to perform the banking transactions.

The second reason for preparation of a financial POA is preventative in nature. If you lose the mental capacity to handle your own financial affairs without a durable power of attorney (see below), your family members will need to go to court and have a guardian or conservator appointed over your assets. If you have previously set up a durable power of attorney and then lose mental capacity, the agent named in your POA will be able to handle your financial affairs without the time and attorney fees necessary for going to the court to get a guardian and conservator appointed.

A *"durable"* POA is one that remains in force even after the principal (i.e. the individual who executed the POA) loses mental capacity. Unless a POA is "durable," it will become ineffective at the time the principal becomes incompetent. Thus, a POA which is not "durable" fails to protect you against the potential of your family having to go to court and get a guardian and conservator appointed over your assets.

What Makes a Power of Attorney "Durable"?

This is a matter of state law. The Uniform Durable Power of Attorney Act has been adopted by 48 states and provides the following definition:

> *"A durable power of attorney is a power of attorney by which a principal, in writing, designates another as his attorney in fact and the writing contains the words, 'This power of attorney shall not be affected by subsequent disability or incapacity of the principal', or 'This power of attorney shall become effective upon the disability or incapacity of the principal', or similar words showing the intent of the principal that the authority conferred shall continue notwithstanding the subsequent disability or incapacity of the principal."*

Therefore, the first requirement is that there be a written and signed document, and second, that the document contains words such as those above which clearly indicate that the principal intended the POA to be effective even after he or she became incapacitated. Although the language of the Uniform Act does not specifically state whether the document must also be notarized in order to be durable, the form recommended by the Uniform Law Commission has a space for the signature of a notary. Most states require POAs to be notarized to be durable, and for them to be effective for real estate transactions. It is recommended that your POA be notarized. Also, some states require witnesses to the principal's signature.

Advanced Directives (Living Wills)

Any healthcare professional will tell you that having an advanced directive (living will) may be the most important document you ever put together in your entire life. Having an advanced directive helps adult children, or any loved one, understand your wishes for the end of your life when you are no longer able to communicate those wishes yourself.

The term "advanced directive" refers to legal means by which individuals can express and, within certain limits, enforce their wishes regarding health care in the event that they become unconscious or otherwise mentally incapacitated. Common examples include living wills (which may direct families and physicians to withhold or withdraw life support if the person is terminally ill and for permanently unconscious) and durable powers of attorney (which appoint and invest third parties with full authority to make decisions regarding healthcare for incapacitated patients). When properly set up, these documents provide those who, in good faith, follow their provisions with protection from prosecution and civil suit.

A good elder law attorney (**www.naela.org**) can assist you and your family members draft an advanced directive, and most hospitals today will provide the forms and notaries for you upon admission to the hospital.

Five Wishes

One example of an advanced directive is called "Five Wishes." The Five Wishes document helps you express how you want to be treated if you are seriously ill and unable to speak for yourself. It is unique among all other living will and health agent forms because it looks to all of a person's needs: medical, personal, emotional and spiritual. Five Wishes also encourages discussing your wishes with your family and physician. Additional information can be found at **www.agingwithdignity.org**

Five Wishes Lets Your Family and Doctors Know:

- Which person you want to make health care decisions for you when you cannot make them.
- The kind of medical treatment you want or do not want.
- How comfortable you want to be.
- How you want people to treat you.
- What you want your loved ones to know.

Revocable Living Trust

This is a trust created by an individual (the trustor), and administered by another party (the trustee), while the trustor is still alive. The individual creating the living trust can be his or her own trustee while they are living and not incapacitated. Upon the individual's death, a successor trustee named in the trust will become the administrator. A living trust can be either revocable or irrevocable. At the time of death, a living trust avoids probate in court and therefore gets assets of the estate distributed much more quickly and with less cost than a will does. It also offers a higher level of confidentiality, as probate proceedings are a matter of public record. Additionally, trusts are usually harder to contest than wills.

On the downside, a living trust takes longer to put together than a will, and requires more ongoing maintenance. Although both a will and a living trust can be modified or revoked at any time before death, such changes are slightly more time-consuming for a living trust. Additionally, assets that a person wants to move to a living trust, such as real estate and bank or brokerage accounts, have to be re-titled in the name of the trust.

Irrevocable Trusts

An irrevocable trust is an arrangement in which the grantor departs with ownership and control of property. Usually this involves a gift of the property to the trust. The trust then stands as a separate taxable entity and pays tax on its accumulated income. Trusts typically receive a deduction for income that is distributed on a current basis. Because the grantor must permanently depart with the ownership and control of the property being transferred to an irrevocable trust, such a device has limited appeal to most taxpayers.

Homes that have been put into an irrevocable trust are generally not eligible for a reverse mortgage. An irrevocable trust is typically used in very advanced estate-planning strategies.

How to Use Medicaid to Pay for Long-Term Care

While Medicaid should be used as a last resort to pay for long-term care, there are two cases where this may be the only option for a family to protect assets. The first example is a married couple. In the case of a married couple, the federal law allows for a division of assets to occur at the time that either spouse enters a nursing home. Simply put, the couple is able to divide their assets by two and the healthy spouse, usually considered the community spouse, is able to keep half of the assets up to $148,6201.[1] Put another way, let's assume we have a couple living in Missouri, Mary, age 78, and her husband, Bill, age 82. Their countable assets total $380,000. Even though when you divide the assets by two, you would expect that each spouse would be entitled to $190,000, the healthy spouse, i.e. community spouse, is only able to keep $148,620 in this example. The balance of $231,380 would need to be spent down to $10,603 before Medicaid will begin paying as of 2023.[2] However, if the fam-

---

1   **Medicaid's Community Spouse Resource Allowance** (CSRA): Calculations & Limits American Council on Aging https://www.medicaidplanningassistance.org/community-spouse-resource-allowance/#countable

2   **State Medicaid Figures** The Krause Agency https://thekrauseagency.com/resources/state-resources/

ily is aware of the OBRA 93 (the Omnibus Reconciliation Act of 1993), they would learn that, actually, the healthy spouse can retain the $231,380 by converting this amount into an annuity that is compliant with OBRA 93. While many individuals have annuities, this particular annuity is something that you would only come in contact with if you are in a long-term care crisis and are attempting to do Medicaid or Veterans planning. In order for an annuity to be Medicaid compliant it must be irrevocable, nonassignable, non-commutable, nontransferable and actuarially sound. When properly done, this planning will allow the healthy spouse to maintain 100% of the assets by using an annuity that is compliant with OBRA 93 (See Exhibit 13.1).

Exhibit 13.1

Medicaid Spend-Down 101

ALL Assets from Both Spouses Fit into 1 of 3 Categories:

Exempt Assets	Countable Assets	Unavailable Assets
Principal Residence	Other Real Estate	OBRA '93 Compliant Annuity
Business Property	CDs, Checking, Savings, MM, $380,000	
One Car	Stocks, Bonds, Brokerage	
Personal Contents	Annuities	
Term Life Insurance	IRA	
$1,500 of Cash Value in Whole Life Insurance Policy	Life Insurance Cash Value	
Prepaid funeral	Mutual Funds	

TOTALS: *$380,000*

Illustration for Immediate Medicaid Qualification

Total Countable Assets............. **$380,000**

Division of Assets.......................Divisible by 2

Each Spouse's Share of Assets.... **$190,000**

Maximum Amount of Countable Assets Community Spouse Can Keep Is $148,620

$380,000

	Bill: Nursing Home	Mary: Community Spouse
	$231,380	**$148,620**

Spend down to $10,603 by privately paying for Bill's care at $7,000 monthly, the asset will be depleted in 38 months.

OR

Purchase OBRA '93 Medicaid compliant annuity for Mary. This will allow Bill to qualify immediately for Medicaid and Mary will have protected the entire $380,000.

Use $231,380 to Purchase Medicaid Compliant Immediate Annuity in Mary's Name

Produces a Total of $2,173 (Plus Interest) Monthly Income to Mary for 10 Years

Examples are hypothetical. Results are not guaranteed. Consult a tax or financial professional.

The case of a single individual using Medicaid as a long-term care planning strategy is a little more challenging. However, it may make sense to consider whether or not the family is concerned about making sure that there are adequate funds to pay for their parent's funeral expenses and other expenses that are not covered by Medicaid. Under current Medicaid rules, an individual may be able to transfer approximately 25-50% of the assets to their children or possibly into an irrevocable trust. The balance would be deposited into annuity that is compliant with OBRA 93. The income generated from the annuity, along with Social Security and pension income, would pay for the cost of care during the penalty period that was created by making a transfer of the other 25-50%. Put another way, let's use Edith, age 80, who recently entered a nursing home where they have Medicaid beds available. Since Edith has an IRA worth $150,000, and an additional $150,000 in her money market and checking accounts she would be unable to qualify for Medicaid. However, if we transferred her $150,000 to a properly drafted irrevocable trust and the remaining balance of $150,000 IRA into an annuity, the income from this IRA annuity, along with her Social Security and pension, would allow her to privately pay during the penalty that was created by transferring the other $150,000 into the trust. As a result, Edith would be eligible to receive Medicaid benefits after the penalty of only 31 months. The end result is that Edith has now protected half of her assets, or $150,000, for her future needs and the future of her children (See Exhibit 13.2).

Exhibit 13.2

Medicaid Spend Down 101

ALL Assets from Both Spouses Fit into 1 of 3 Categories:

Exempt Assets	Countable Assets	Unavailable Assets
Principal Residence	Other Real Estate	OBRA '93 Compliant Annuity
Business Property	CDs, Checking, Savings, MM, $150,000	
One Car	EE Bonds	
Personal Contents	Annuities	
Term Life Insurance	IRA – $150,000	
$1,500 of Cash Value in Whole Life Insurance Policy	Mutual Funds, Stocks, Bonds	
Prepaid funeral	Cash Value Life Insurance	

TOTALS: *$300,000*

Exhibit 13.2 continued on the next page …

Asset Protection Plan

Exhibit 13.2

Current Situation

Countable Assets $300,000

**$50,000
Checking**

**$150,000
IRA**

**$100,000
Money
Market**

Monthly Cost..................................... $9,000
Less Income .... – $2,500
Monthly Shortfall .... ($6,500)

*Due to current countable assets exceeding $5,035,
Edith would not be able to apply for Medicaid and would deplete
100% of assets in approximately 6 years.*

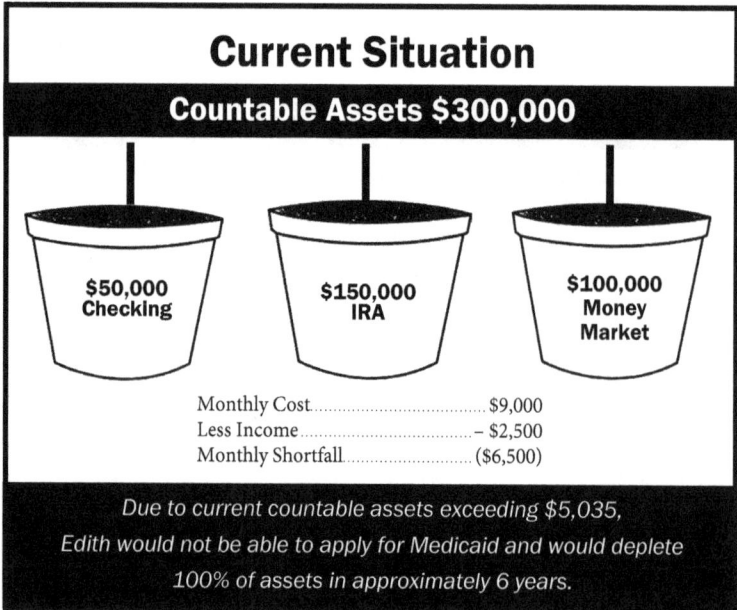

Examples are hypothetical. Results are not guaranteed. Consult a tax or financial professional.

Asset Protection Plan

Exhibit 13.2

Proposed

Countable Assets $5,035

Transfer $150,000 IRA to IRA using OBRA '93 annuity for 23.2 months to cover shortfall during penalty period.

$50,000 Checking

$150,000 IRA

$100,000 Money Market

KEEP $5,035 Checking

Monthly Cost	$9,000
Less Income	– $2,500
Monthly Shortfall	$6,500
OBRA '93 IRA for 23.2 months	$6,500
Net monthly Amount needed	$0

Irrevocable Trust
$44,965 Checking | $100,000 Money Market

OUTCOME: Medicaid eligibility is established in 23.2 months and $144,965 of assets are protected.

Examples are hypothetical. Results are not guaranteed. Consult a tax or financial professional.

How to Use Veterans Benefits to Pay for Long-Term Care

The Veterans' Administration offers a special pension with the Aid and Attendance (A&A) Benefit that is largely unknown. This Special Pension allows for Veterans and surviving spouses who require the regular attendance of another person to assist in eating, bathing, dressing, undressing, or taking care of the needs of nature to receive additional monetary benefits. It also includes individuals who are blind or a patient in a nursing home because of mental or physical incapacity. It is not a benefit for a person needing housekeeping or respite or part-time care. Assisted care in an assisted-living facility or even at home also qualifies. This most important benefit is overlooked by many families with veterans or surviving spouses who need additional monies to help care for ailing parents or loved ones. This is a "pension benefit" and is not dependent upon service-related injuries for compensation. Many veterans who are in need of assistance qualify for this pension. Always seek professional advice when considering this type of assistance.

This special pension benefit addresses the needs of veterans and their surviving spouses who have non-service related disabilities and who require regular assistance with the activities of daily living.

In order for a veteran to qualify for this benefit, he or she must have served 90 days of active duty with one day of active service during a defined period of war.

The following are the VA's defined "periods of war":

- **WWI: 4/16/1917 to 11/11/1918**
- **WWII: 12/7/1941 to 12/31/1946**
- **Korea: 6/25/1950 to 1/31/1955**
- **Vietnam: 8/5/1964 to 5/7/1975**
- **Persian Gulf: 8/2/90 to present**

Who benefits from VA LTC benefit? Tale of Two Veterans.

Let's consider an example with two veterans. They both served in WWII at the Battle of the Bulge, worked thirty plus years together with the same employer, and ended up down the hall from each other in the same assisted living apartment complex. However, they led very different lives.

1. Veteran number one followed the wine, women and song approach to life. He had three divorces, the bars and casino knew him by first name, and he had $35k to his name.

2. Veteran number two stayed married to the same woman for forty plus years, had three daughters and had $460k in his name.

Who should get the VA Pension? What do you think?

We say both served and neither should be discriminated against due to lifestyle. We should not discriminate against the veteran who led a less than perfect life nor should we discriminate against the middle class wartime veteran who paid his taxes and contributed to our country. Both put their life on the line during a wartime period and both deserve the benefit.

Do you agree? Who would benefit the most?

This question is not as easy as one might think at first blush.

What do you think?

1. In this case Veteran number one ran out of money in less than a year. He took his new girlfriend and went to a casino. He lost $17k in one weekend. With an Assisted Living Facility, if you do not pay, you do not stay. His family was told he needed to leave, and the family will need to take care of him. In many cases this is what happens. In this case none of his ex-wives' or children were willing to help him at all. The new "girlfriend" found a new boyfriend. He was forced to go to a nursing home 50 miles out of town that would accept him on Medicaid. No one visited him, he hated the nursing home, and he lost his VA pension. If you are not paying your bill and Medicaid is paying, you are not allowed to "double dip. His $1800+ monthly pension was reduced to a $90 per month allotment. He was very angry at losing his pension and being forced into a nursing home.

2. Veteran number 2, with his additional resources, stayed in the same assisted living apartment for the next 4 1/2 years and NEVER had to go to a nursing home. His family and he were big beneficiaries of his wartime service to the tune of over $117,000 in tax free income.

We take the strong position that every disabled wartime veteran and their widow EARNED their pension with their wartime service. They wrote a check up to and including their life during a wartime period, it is now time for the country to pay back in THEIR time of need.

The truth is that many times the poor end up on Medicaid with only the $90 VA allotment. Middle class wartime veterans/surviving spouses benefit the most since they can get full pension from $1,433 up to $2,643 per month and have other assets to help make up difference. If they have $1,500 to $2,000 in Social Security and maybe a pension, the extra $1,433 to $2,643 per month can double their income. The cost of home care or an assisted living apartment is typically $5,000 per month. The deficit of $1,000 is much more manageable than $3,000 per month. Most of our wartime veterans have between $250,000 and $750,000 in net worth. They are not rich, but they are not poor. The VA Pension is very important to them. Millionaire veterans, though eligible, tend not to have near as much interest as middle class. All wartime veterans/spouse whether rich, poor or in between can be helped, but the middle class veterans, by far, will benefit the most.

Most people incorrectly believe that you must be poor. Sadly, if they go to the VA, they are usually told they are not eligible because they have "too much money." It is not true, but that is typically what they are told. This benefit is not a welfare benefit. On October 18, 2018, the allowed assets were increased. As of 2023, if you have less than $150,538 in total assets, you may be eligible to file if you meet medical expense and medical rating requirements. The amount of monthly income, and the cost of non-reimbursed medical expenses, will determine the maximum amount of benefits.

If planning has been done properly, the Veteran may be eligible for VA Aid and Attendance beginning the first day of the following month. A word of warning is that it is currently taking, in many cases, up to 6-8 months to get a claim approved. In these cases, the VA does provide retroactive payment back to the first day of the month following the application (See Exhibit 14.1).

How Much Does VA Pay?

Aid and Attendance can help pay for care in the home, nursing home or assisted-living facility. In 2023, a veteran is eligible for up to $2,229 per month, while a surviving spouse is eligible for up to $1,433 per month. A couple where a veteran needs care assistance with either two ADLs or a cognitive impairment is eligible for up to $2,643 per month. All income is TAX FREE.

In many cases, if a person has a paid caregiver such as a nurse's aide, or they pay an assisted-living facility, those expenses impact so greatly on a person's net income that they will meet the criteria for the income level.

Most middle-class veterans with assets between $200,000 and $800,000 can receive the benefit with advance planning. So the million-dollar question is, "What should the veteran do if their assets exceed the maximum amount determined by the new VA guidelines?"

If a veteran or veteran's widow has cash assets above the limit, they are allowed to place those assets into certain investments. Given the veteran's age, prudence dictates that three rules should be followed: Safety of Principal, adequate liquidity and better potential return than a bank CD. I have yet to have anyone disagree with the VA Accredited Attorney's three prudent rules. This VA Trust planning does have a 3 year "look-back period" associated with it. For example, a 73-year-old Vietnam Veterans can properly plan and be eligible at 76 or any time thereafter. Unfortunately, procrastination has large cost in VA Planning. For example if you fail to plan until you are 91 years old, you would not be eligible till you are 94! You earned your LTC benefit with your wartime service. The country has provided this benefit as a thank you for your service with funding attached. There is no premium required for this benefit. Proper asset planning for Aid and Attendance should be done under the supervision of an experienced financial professional and VA

Accredited Attorney well versed in Medicaid planning. One could easily ruin the chances of ever getting Medicaid if the VA pension planning was done incorrectly.

With a little professional planning, many veterans and veterans' widows can receive pensions that make a significant difference in the amount of care they receive. After all, the reason for this particular pension is to assure that a veteran or veteran's widow does not live in a substandard environment in their old age. In most cases the veteran or surviving spouse use the income to pay for home care or an assisted living apartment. I find their goal is to stay out of a nursing home. It requires planning as early as possible and takes a little work to apply for this pension, but anything worth having usually does.

Two key questions you need to answer.

1. Do I have a son/daughter I totally trust?
2. In the next 25 years can I envision either my spouse or myself suffering a change of health requiring extended care? (Home care or Assisted Living)

Although you can apply on your own, it is best to seek the advice of a professional. There is no fee to apply and find out if you or a loved one is entitled to these services (See Exhibit 14.1).

Finding Answers

Finding a Care Funding Specialist Who Can Help

If you are struggling with a long-term care crisis for an aging parent, a Care Funding Plan will become your road map on how to pay for home care, assisted living, or nursing home costs in the most tax efficient, cost-effective way possible. As an integral part of the plan, your Care Funding Specialist will investigate all available programs including private funding and government programs to potentially reduce the out-of-pocket expenses for care.

Care Funding Specialist

Here is what you should expect from a qualified Care Funding Specialist who can walk you through the right process:

1. A professional who will clearly define your loved one's care needs and costs.

2. Comprehensive analysis and evaluation of all sources of income, expenses, cash flow, taxes, current asset allocation, economic variables, and health/longevity risks (Care Funding Analysis).

3. Analysis of the facts and creation of a written comprehensive plan in a language that you can understand.

4. Implementation of plan: In an effort to achieve the best results from your Care Funding Plan, the professional will

coordinate their efforts with elder law attorneys if needed, who will help you with the application for Medicaid and veteran benefits when appropriate. Upon implementation of the plan, they should carefully monitor it, and communicate with you on a regular basis through periodic reviews and quarterly performance reports. Your advisor should have considerable experience in Care Funding Plans.

Elder Law Attorneys

Aging adults and their family members face certain challenging legal issues. Issues such as legal matters, financial matters, and care planning can be complicated for seniors, as well as for their family. Once again, expert legal help is often the key to solving many problems and avoiding future complexities. It is important to be able to identify a competent elder law attorney who can assist the family in a timely and professional manner. Consumers should be cautious and check credentials thoroughly.

The leading national organization of elder law attorneys is the National Academy of Elder Law Attorneys (NAELA), on the web at: **www.naela.org.** Membership is open to any lawyer, but the membership does show that at least the attorney has some interest in the field. Other sources to consider are referrals from family and friends, and referrals from other professionals such as social workers and medical professionals who work in long-term care. Ask the attorney how many nursing-home cases they handle each month. It is likely that the attorney who does four Medicaid cases per month is more up to date than the attorney who does four per year.

Legal problems that affect the elderly are growing in number. Our laws and regulations are becoming more complex. Actions taken by older people with regard to a single matter may have unintended legal effects. It is important for attorneys dealing with seniors to have a broad understanding of the laws that may have an impact on a given situation, to avoid future problems.

Elder law attorneys can help with:

- trusts
- wills
- durable powers of attorney
- Medicaid and VA benefits
- advanced medical directives
- other important legal issues and documents

Geriatric Care Managers as a Resource

When faced with decisions regarding long-term care for an aging loved one, a geriatric care manager may be one of the best private resources in your area. A geriatric care manager has extensive knowledge of all local resources related to aging and care-giving, as well as family and personal issues and concerns.

Geriatric care managers can be located nationwide. They assist with coordination of care for aging and disabled adults. This service is provided in a series of steps including initial assessment, care plan development, implementation of services, and quality-of-care monitoring. Geriatric care managers are typically nurses, social workers, gerontologists, physical therapists, occupational therapists, or other social service professionals.

The "care management" process can improve the quality of life not only for the aging adult, but also for the caregivers and family members involved. The service is very personalized and utilizes the same principles of "case management."

Most geriatric care managers are available to the family and client 24 hours per day, 7 days per week. The ultimate goal is to keep the aging adult in the home for as long as safely possible. In-home care can be arranged at any level of need to accommodate the client and the family. Geriatric care managers often will be asked to arrange other services for the client, such as bill paying, housekeeping, lawn care, transportation to appointments, grocery shopping, meal delivery, and personal care.

When the client is in need of transition to alternative living arrangements, such as a nursing home, assisted living, or even an independent retirement community, the care manager can often recommend the best facilities to meet the client's financial needs.

Geriatric care management is truly a holistic approach to caring for the aging adult. All resources available are utilized to assist families when long-term care is needed.

Care managers are also often asked to troubleshoot quality concerns with nursing homes and home-care agencies. Their level of professionalism and knowledge of the local regulations and laws are of great value to the family. They are considered "advocates" for the elderly.

Geriatric care management is paid for privately by client and family members. Medicare and Medicaid do not cover these services. However, long-term care insurance does cover some or all of the care management fee.

Most geriatric care managers belong to the National Association of Professional Geriatric Care Managers. In order to find a care manager in your area, you can search for one through their website at **www.aginglifecare.org.**

Recommendations for Choosing a Geriatric Care Manager

Choosing a geriatric care manager is much like choosing any other professional that you and your family would be working with closely.

- Look for a member of the National Association of Professional Geriatric Care Managers. These members have met certain criteria regarding education and experience in health sciences and social service.

- Ask for references.
- Ask for literature about their company, years of practice, websites, and biography.
- Check with the Better Business Bureau.
- Ask about fees, contracts, and extra charges like mileage or phone calls.
- Be sure you understand what services they provide and their on-call schedule. Will they be available 24 hours a day?
- Remember that a geriatric care manager becomes your "eyes and ears," especially when you live some distance from your parents. Ask them about their process and their communication schedule (Will they report daily, weekly, or monthly?). Is the primary communication via telephone or email?
- Communicate any concerns immediately, and work together as a team to accomplish the ultimate goal, which is keeping your loved one safe and well cared for.

My Parent Doesn't Want Any Help, What Should I Do?

Perhaps you have noticed that Mom or Dad is not bathing regularly, or the bills are not being paid, or the house is uncharacteristically messy. Maybe they seem to forget directions from one location to another, or even worse, they have had a car accident, or report falling in the home when no one was around to help them. Often adult children of aging parents notice changes in their loved ones, and when the aging adult is confronted with the facts, they say, "Oh everything is fine, I don't need any help, don't worry about me!"

The loss of independence and choice is something no one wants to face. Having one's own children tell them what to do or how to live their lives is uncomfortable at best. Many aging adults are also very private about their financial matters and will not discuss income, expenses, or assets with adult children.

How Does an Adult Child Start That Conversation with Their Parents?

There is not a one-size-fits-all answer. Below are some tips that might help the process along.

- Choose an appropriate time and place. Avoid large family gatherings, holidays, birthdays, and other celebrations. A quiet location, in their home or yours, might be more comfortable.
- Avoid blaming or accusing. Instead, redirect the conversation by telling your parent how YOU feel. For example, "Mom, I find myself worrying about you a lot these days, and I would like to tell you why I am feeling this way."
- Talk to a geriatric care manager in your area for some good advice on how to approach your parent's specific needs. That care manager has helped family members have this kind of conversation hundreds of times throughout their career. They are full of helpful hints and tips.
- If you decide to seek the services of a geriatric care manager, ask them about their approach when it comes to dealing with difficult clients or clients who may not perceive a need for services.
- Advice for adult children when approaching their parents about setting up an evaluation might include telling their parents, "I know you don't want me to worry about you, and I only want the best for you. Having this professional come over and talk to us would really make me feel better.

If you would agree to talk with her, we can look at her recommendations together and see if any of them make sense. Is that fair?"

- Remember that having a third party who is not a family member and is completely objective can help the senior see things from a different point of view. They feel like they are getting some professional advice as opposed to opinions from their children.

Finally, if the senior is truly not living safely, a geriatric care manager can let the senior know that they need to make some choices about their care or living arrangements NOW, before someone else has to make that decision for them later. Of course, this is done with professionalism, courtesy, compassion and caring.

Conclusion

It comes as no surprise to anyone that the family dynamic in America has changed over the years. Seniors often worry about outliving their money and what would happen if they ever really did need expensive long-term care!? Economics demand that most of us of "working age" have two-income families, and we find ourselves busy with our children's extra-curricular activities. Furthermore, most of us with aging family members have had that thought in the back of our minds more than once: "What are we going to do with/ for Mom and Dad when the time comes where they can no longer care for themselves?"

Most seniors today live independently or at home with some form of assistance coming in to attend to their needs. Only 35% of seniors who need care are actually in nursing homes, while 65% are cared for in a home-like setting.[1]

Every stage of our lives brings with it changes, fears, obstacles, questions, wonders, opportunities, happy times, and not-so-happy times. Seniors will tell you that their greatest fears are losing their autonomy, dignity, respect, and independence. Above all else, they are afraid of outliving their money and being put in a nursing home for their remaining days.

---

1 **How Much Care will you Need?** LongTermCare.gov, https://acl.gov/ltc/basic-needs/ how-much-care-will-you-need

Everyone wants to live at home for life. I have yet to meet an aging adult who will tell you that they ultimately prefer to live in a nursing home. For some the process is inevitable. There may come a time for many of us when care at home becomes impossible, mainly for safety or economic reasons.

Although in-home care is less costly than nursing-home care, 24/7 in-home care is difficult for most families to afford to pay for privately. In Tennessee, 24/7 care exceeds the cost of a nursing home if there is no in-home medical required. If medical care is needed, the cost will be much higher. Long-term care insurance is one solu¬tion to keeping seniors safe and at home for longer periods of time. Planning ahead for long-term care has never been a more important concept. However, for some seniors and their families, it is either too late (poor health), or too expensive to afford long-term care insurance.

There are other solutions and ways to manage the crisis of long-term care needs for seniors. There are ways that seniors can help themselves, and families can rest easier knowing that Mom and Dad will be taken care of with the dignity and respect they deserve. All of this can now happen at home for much longer periods of time. Education empowers consumers to remain independent for as long as possible. Talk with each other about long-term care issues and concerns in your family before a crisis happens.

Resources

The following listings are resources available to seniors and their family members nationwide.

Reverse Mortgage Information and Services

National Reverse Mortgage Lenders Association

1400 16th St., NW, Suite 420

Washington, DC 20036

202.939.1760

www.nrmlaonline.org

Long-Term Care Insurance/ Health Insurance

Weiss Ratings, Inc.

4400 Northcorp Pkwy

Palm Beach Gardens, FL 33410

1-877-934-7778

www.weissratings.com

Financial ratings on long-term care insurance companies can be found here.

National Association of Insurance Commissioners—NAIC

Hall of States, 444 North Capitol Street, NW, Suite 701

Washington, DC 20001-1512

202.624.7790 (Voice)

www.naic.org

American Association of Health Plans

601 Pennsylvania Avenue NW, South Building, Suite 500

Washington, DC 20004

202.778.3200

www.ahip.org

American Association of Long-Term Care Insurance

AALTCI, 3835 E. Thousand Oaks Blvd. Suite 336

Westlake Village, CA 91362

818.597.3227

www.aaltci.org

Government Agencies of Interest

Department of Veterans Affairs (VA)

810 Vermont Ave. NW

Washington, DC 20420

800.827.1000

www.va.gov

Paralyzed Veterans of America (PVA)

Veterans Benefits Dept., 801 18th St., NW

Washington, DC 20006

800.424.8200

www.pva.org

Centers for Medicare & Medicaid Services (CMS)
800.MEDICARE
www.medicare.gov

Centers for Medicare and Medicaid Services (CMS),
(formerly the Health Care Financing Administration—CMS)
7500 Security Boulevard
Baltimore, MD 21244

question@cms.gov

www.cms.gov

US Aging
1100 New Jersey Avenue, SE, Suite 350
Washington, DC 20003

202.872.0888

www.n4a.org

Administration on Community Living Eldercare Locator
www.eldercare.acl.gov

National Institute on Aging
www.nia.nih.gov

National Council on Aging
251 18th Street South, Suite 500
Arlington, VA 22202

571.527.3900

www.ncoa.org

Legal Resources

National Academy of Elder Law Attorneys

1577 Sprin Hill Road, Suite 310

Vienna, Virginia 22182

www.naela.org

Caregiver Resources: Home Care and Adult Day Care

National Adult Day Services Association, Inc.

11350 Random Hills Road, Suite 800

Fairfax, VA 22030

Toll Free Phone: 1.877.745.1440

www.nadsa.org

National Association for Home Care and Hospice

228 7th Street, SE

Washington, DC 20003

202.547.7424

www.nahc.org

Caregiver Resources: Hospice

National Hospice and Palliative Care Organization

1731 King Street

Alexandria, Virginia 22314

703.837.1500

www.nhpco.org

Hospice Foundation of America
1707 L Street NW, Suite 220
Washington DC 20036

800.854.3402

www.hospicefoundation.org

Caregiver Resources: Housing

National Shared Housing Resource Center
www.nationalsharedhousing.org

National Center for Assisted Living—NCAL
www.ahcancal.org

Leading Age
2519 Connecticut Ave. NW
Washington, DC 20008

202.783.2242

Caregiver Resources: Geriatric Care Management

Aging Life Care Association
1747 Pennsylvania Avenue NW, Suite 1000
Washington, DC 20006

www.aginglifecare.org

Caregiver Resources: Medications

American Pharmacists Association (APhA)
2215 Constitution Avenue, NW
Washington, DC 20037

202.628.4410

www.pharmacist.com

Center Watch—Clinical Drug Trials Listings
www.centerwatch.com

MEDLINEplus
https://medlineplus.gov/

Caregiver Resources: Finding Doctors

American Medical Association—AMA
www.ama-assn.org

Gerontological Society of America
www.geron.org

Caregiver Resources: Caregiver Organizations and Support

Caregiver Action Network
1150 Connecticut Ave., Suite 501
Washington, DC 20036

202.454.3970

www.caregiveraction.org

Well Spouse Foundation

63 West Main Street—Suite H

Freehold, NJ 07728

732.577.8899

www.wellspouse.org

Other Caregiver Sites of Interest

www.caregiver.com

www.carescout.com

Senior Advocacy and Interest Groups

Families USA

www.familiesusa.org

Alliance for Retired Americans

815 16th Street, NW, 4th floor

Washington, DC 20006

202.637.5399

www.retiredamericans.org

American Society on Aging—ASA

www.asaging.org

Alliance for Aging Research

2021 K Street, NW, Suite 305

Washington, DC 20006

202.293.2856

info@agingresearch.org

www.agingresearch.org

AARP
www.aarp.org

Benefits Check-Up
www.benefitscheckup.org

Miscellaneous Sites of Interest

Mayo Clinic
www.mayoclinic.org

On Health
www.webmd.com

Specific Disease Processes and Organizations On-Line:

National Alzheimer's Association
www.alz.org

Alzheimer's Research Forum
www.alzforum.org

American Cancer Society
www.cancer.org

American Diabetes Association
www.diabetes.org

American Heart Association
www.americanheart.org

American Stroke Association
A Division of American Heart Association
www.strokeassociation.org

Arthritis Foundation
www.arthritis.org

National Organization for Rare Disorders
www.rarediseases.org

National Association for Continence
www.nafc.org

National Osteoporosis Foundation
www.nof.org

National Sleep Foundation
www.sleepfoundation.org

Parkinson's Resource Organization
www.parkinsonsresource.org

Hearing Loss Association of America
www.hearingloss.com

Lighthouse Guild
www.lighthouseguild.org

About the Author

KERRY MORRIS, CFP®, CFED® is the founder of of HonorShield, LLC., a firm he launched to challenge the current thinking and behavior of consumers and financial advisors around preparing for the potential high cost of aging. He has spent several of his twenty-five year career advising hundreds of families experiencing the nightmare of paying for care. The question, always, was "how to make the money last"? The answer would lead him to discover a whole new way to approach and solve this problem: the LCAP—the Longevity Care Allocation Plan.

Morris learned the value of hard work watching his dad, a truck driver, and his mom, a secretary, provide a solid middle-class childhood for him and his sister in and around Nashville TN in the late 60's and 70's. He got his first job when he was fourteen, making $2.75 an hour taking care of baseball fields, and he's never looked back. As he worked his way through high school and university, playing multiple sports, and then spending almost ten years in the TN National Guard and Army Reserve, he developed a respect for the hard work it took any family to build and maintain a nest egg for their future. He honors those efforts with every plan he builds for his clients.

As a Certified Financial Planner™ professional, he has watched too many families, too many men and women, not be fully prepared for retirement. There had to be a better way, a win-win solution that more American's could feel good about embracing. But there was another problem: he witnessed time and again how the financial industry had this issue on total "ignore" mode, often shoving it onto a small-but valiant band of traditional "insurance specialists" around the country. Less than 10% of Americans have ever embraced this model. That is a problem for American families and our country.

Every person, every family deserves to know how an LCAP works. Kerry Morris has made it his life's goal to ensure that those he helps can hold their head high and know that no matter what curve balls retirement throws at them, they will be prepared.